Sugar Skulls Coloring Book

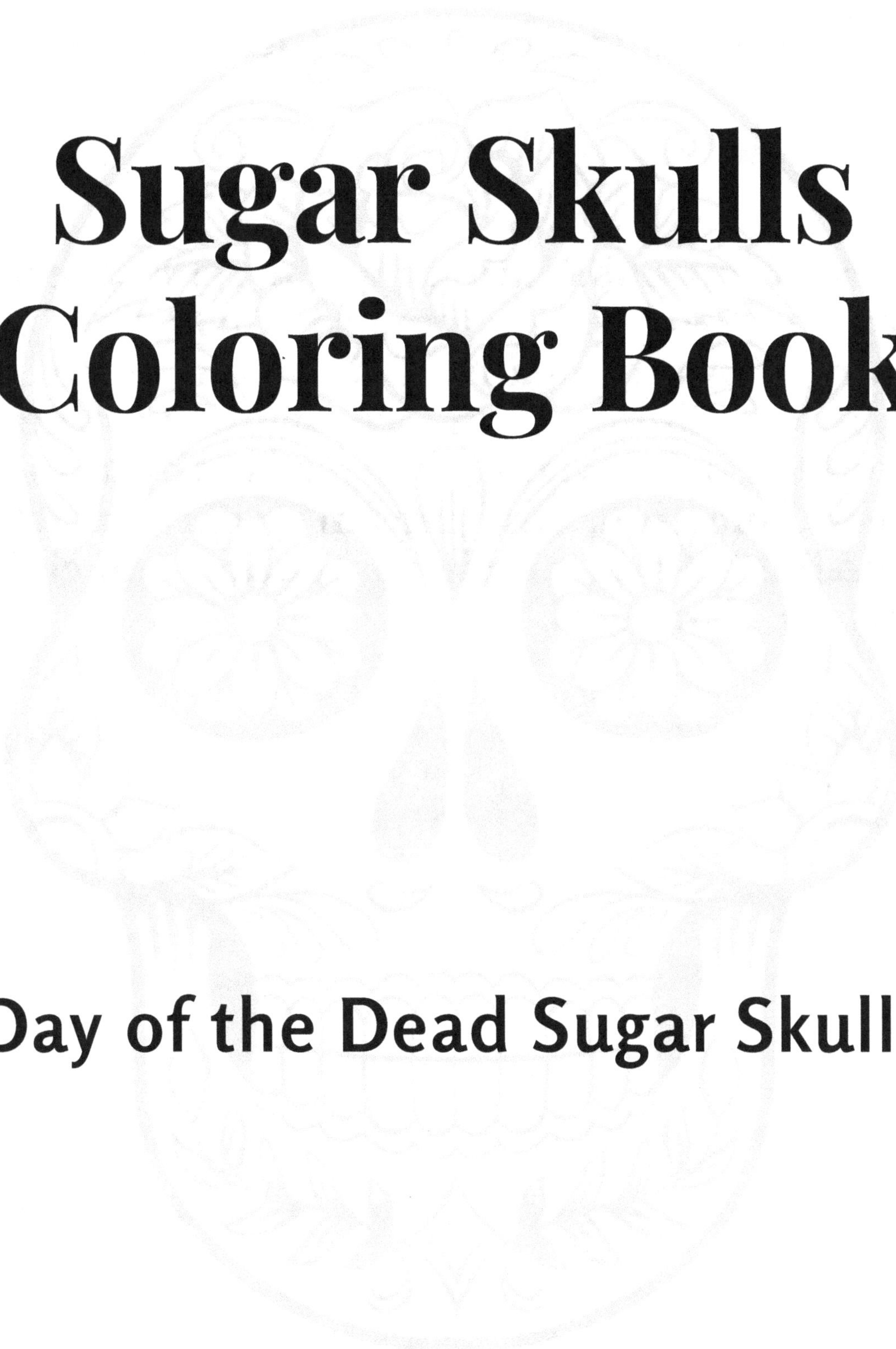

Day of the Dead Sugar Skulls

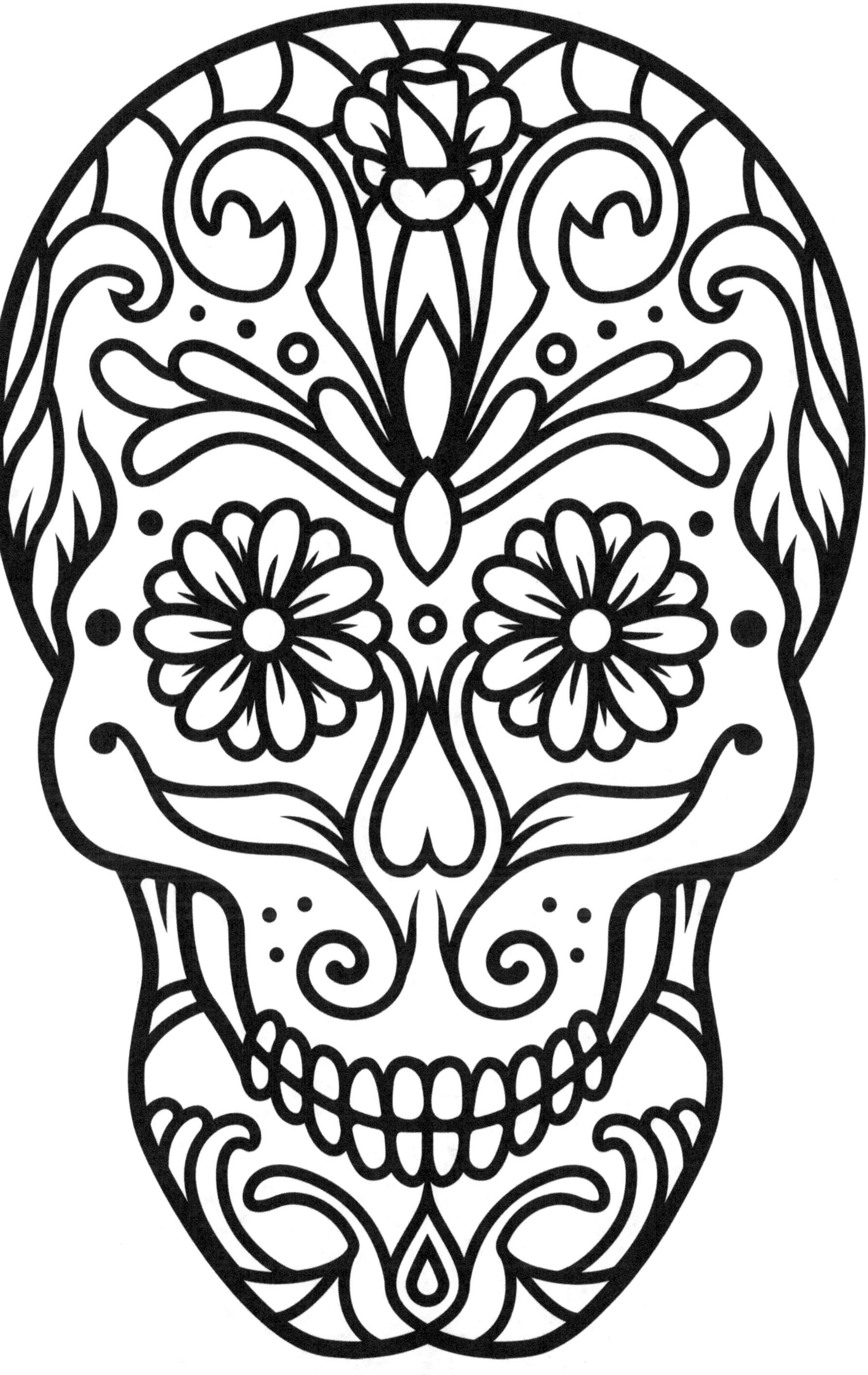

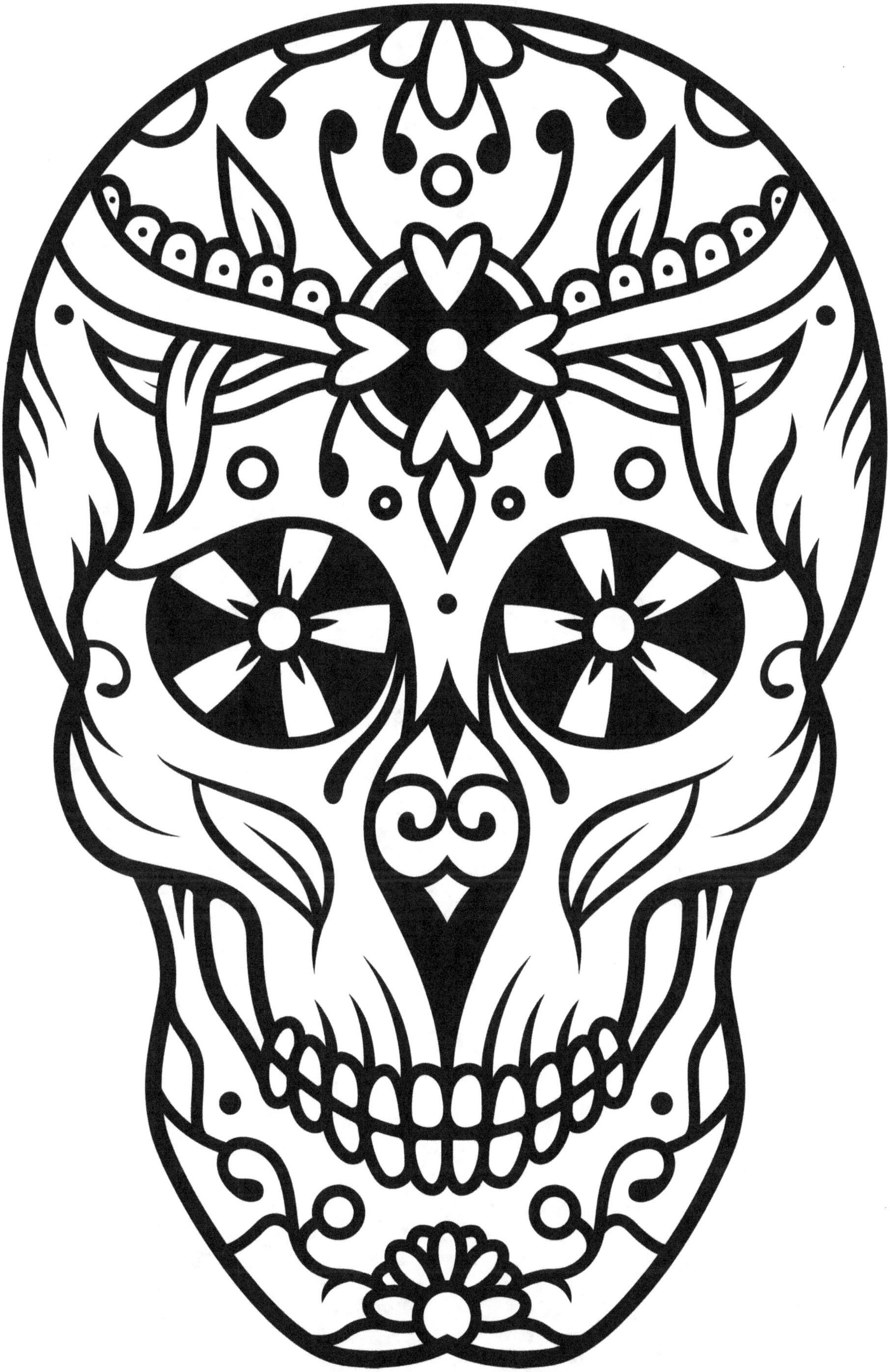

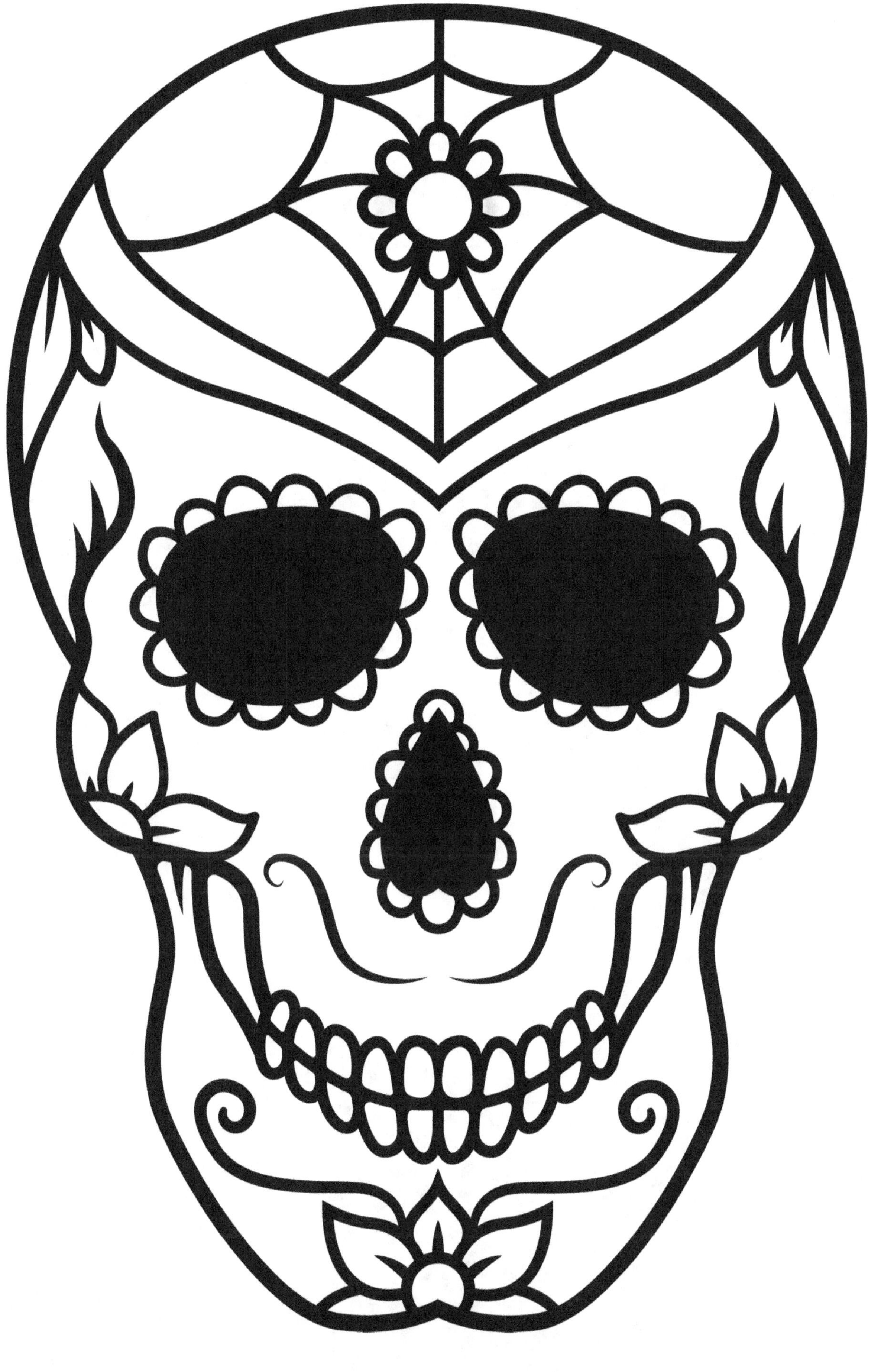

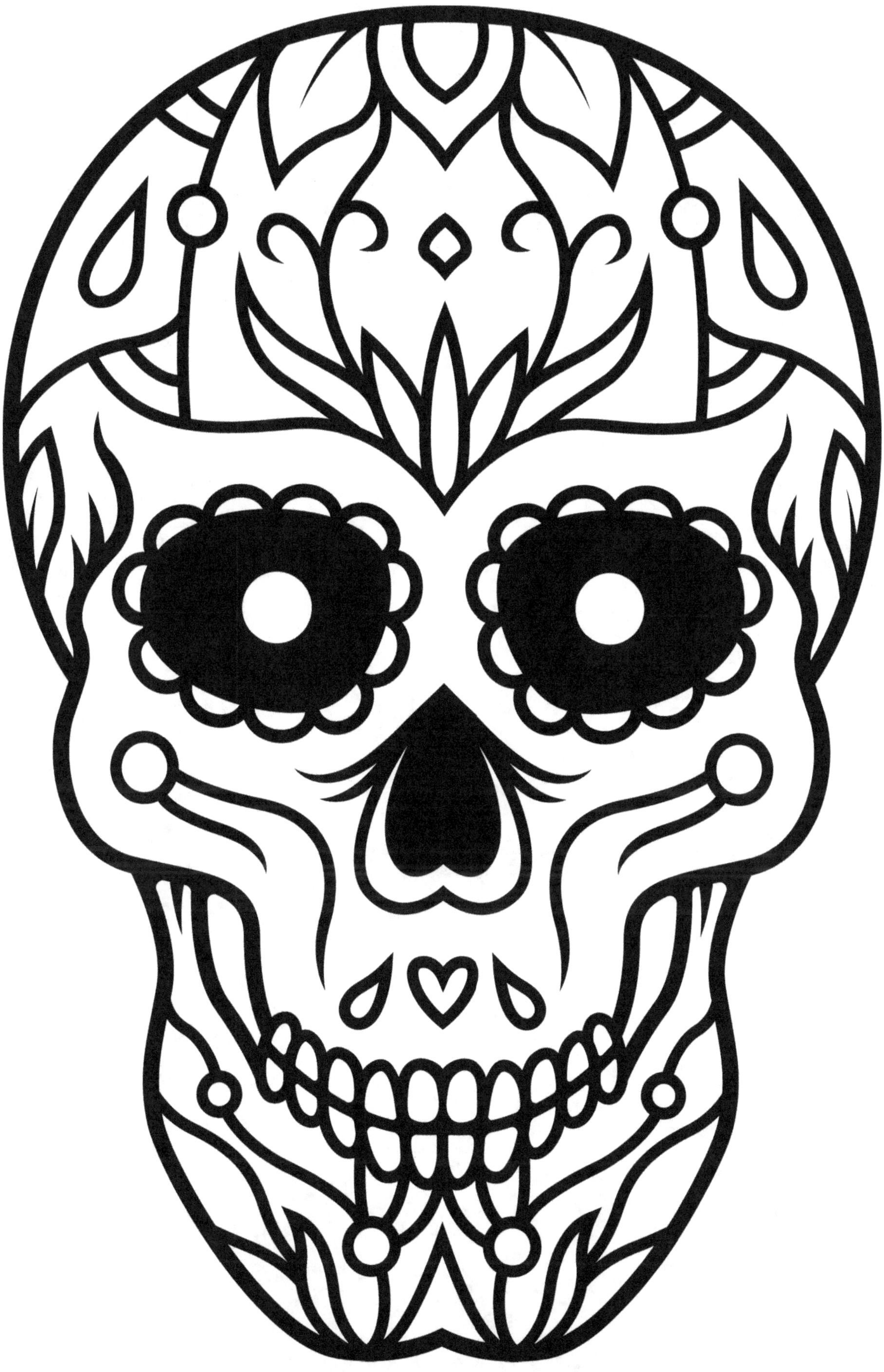

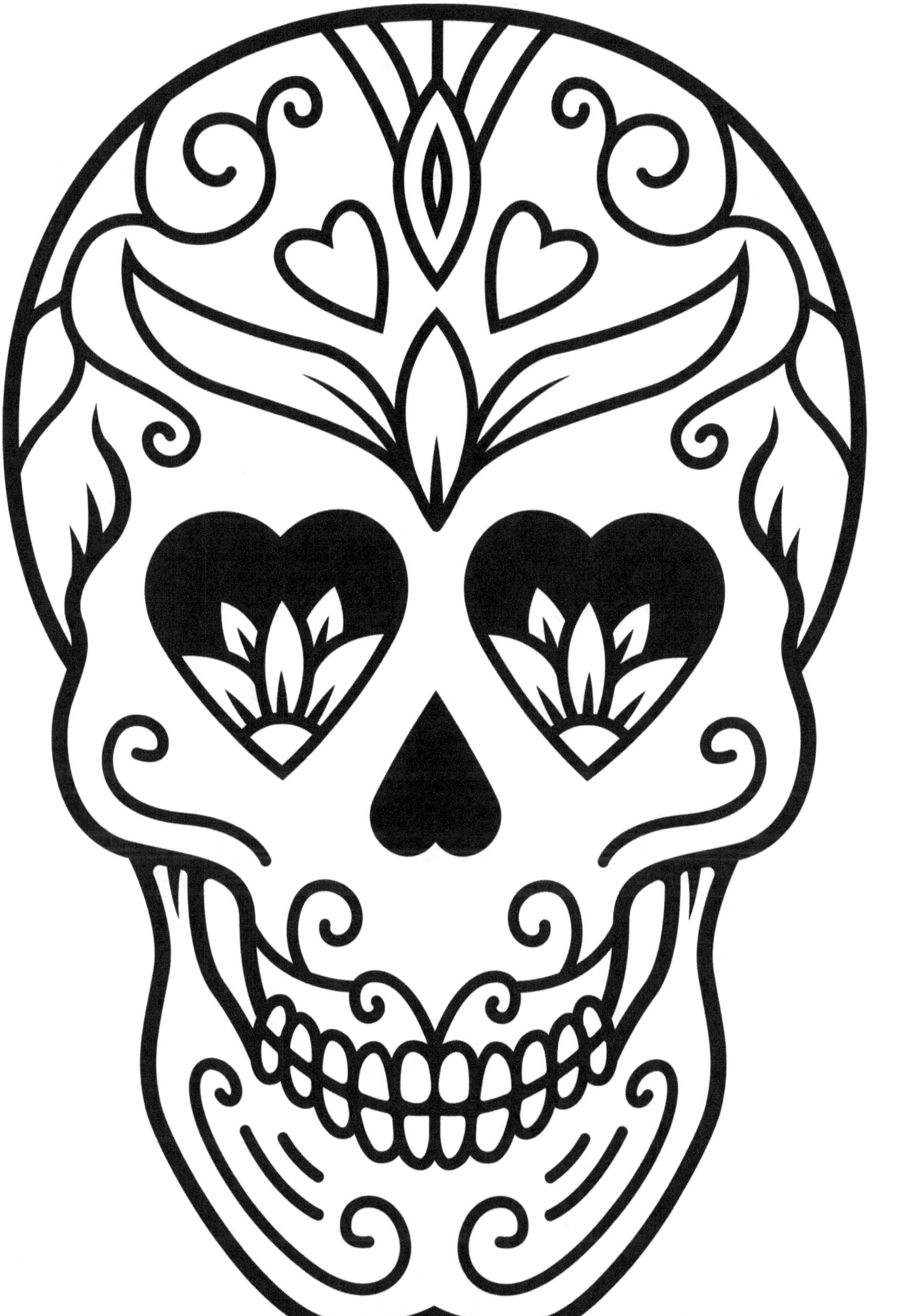

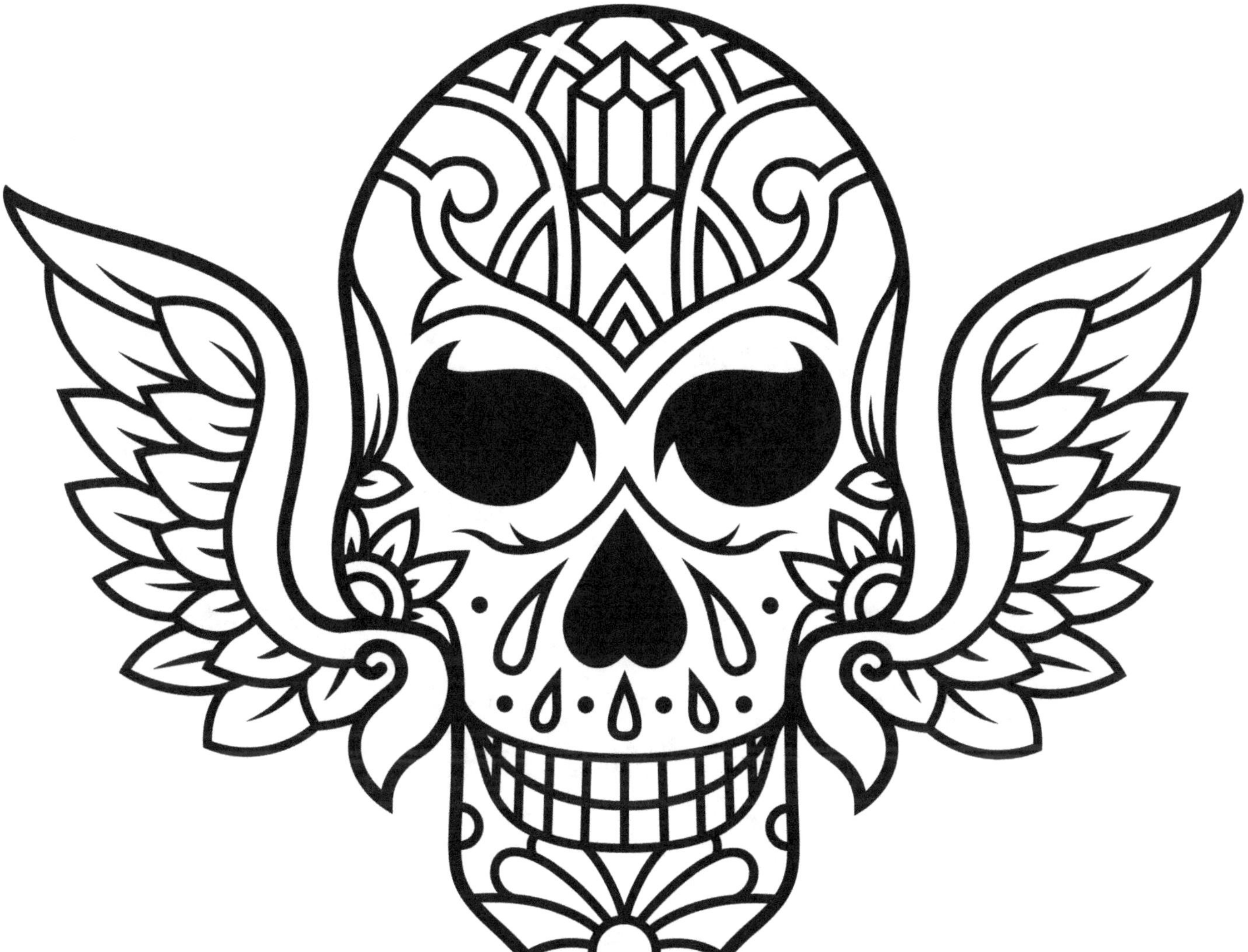

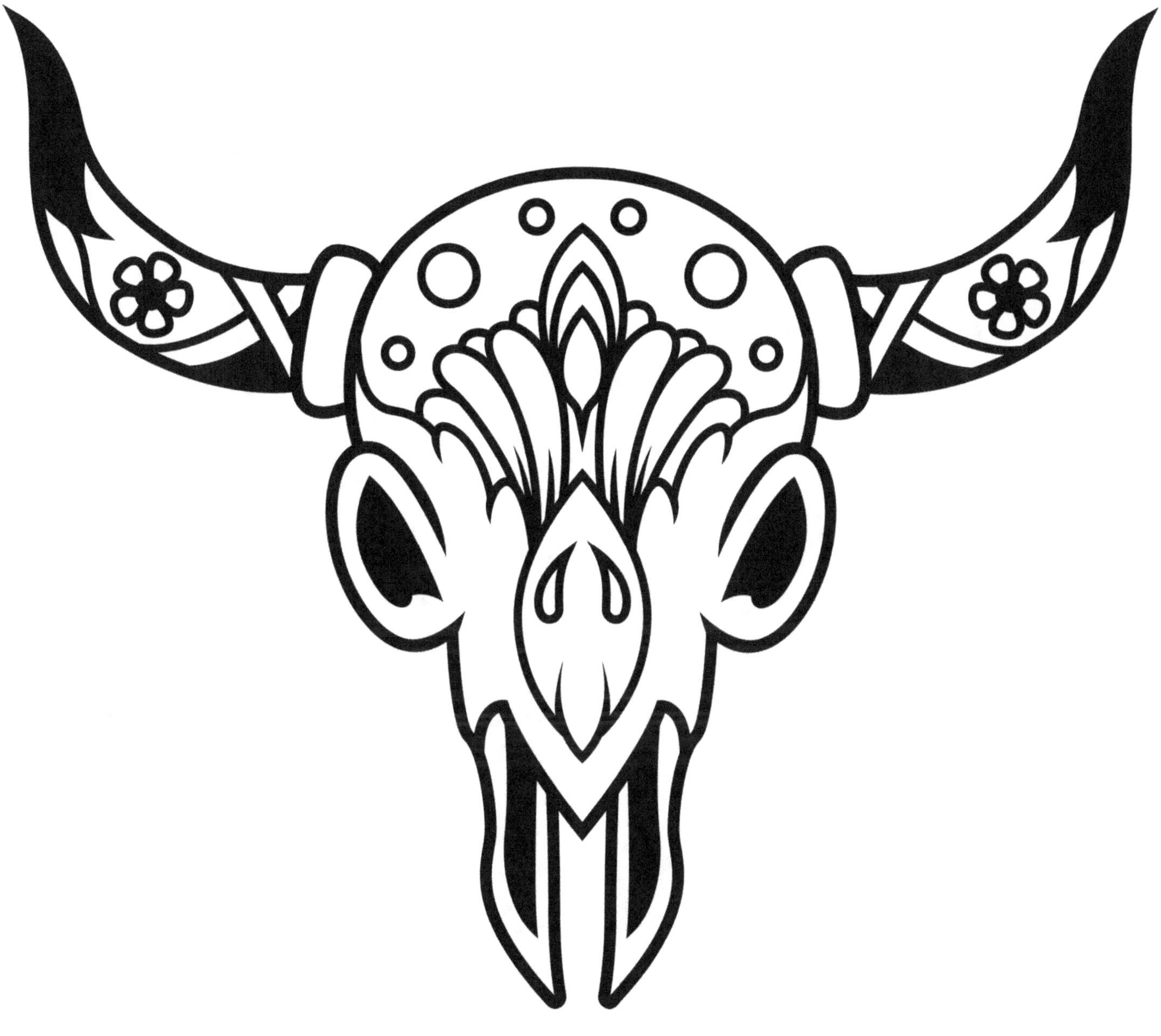

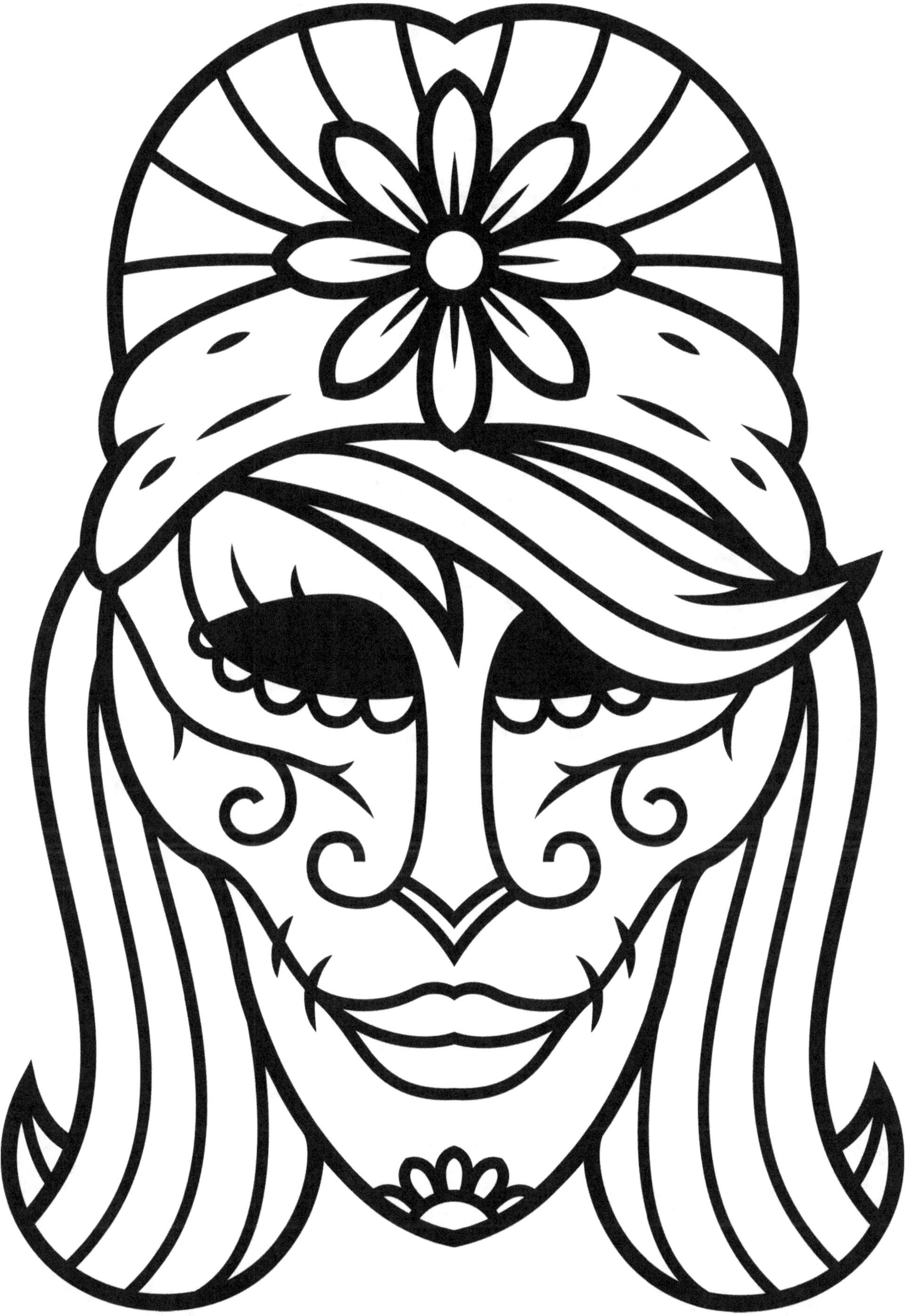

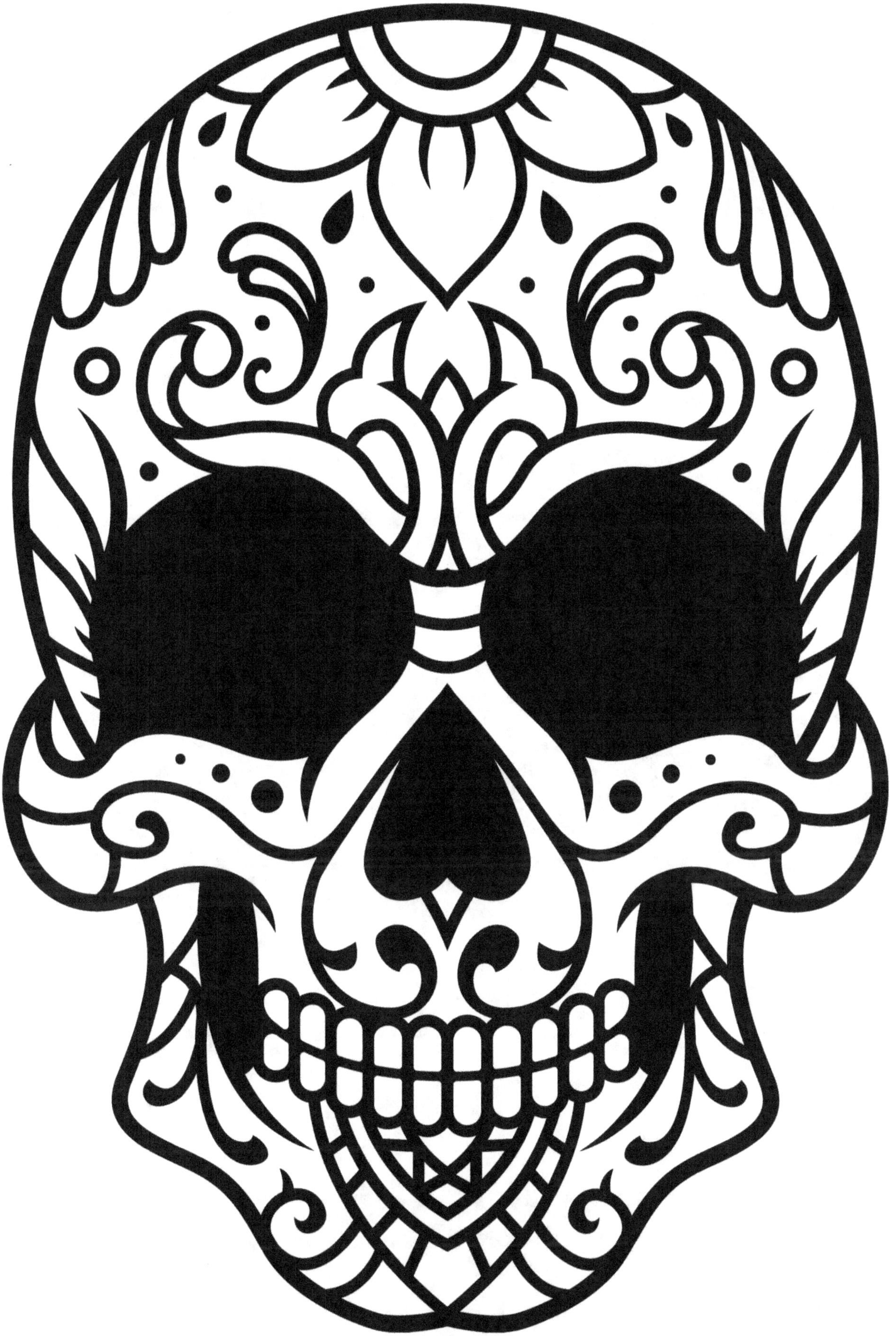

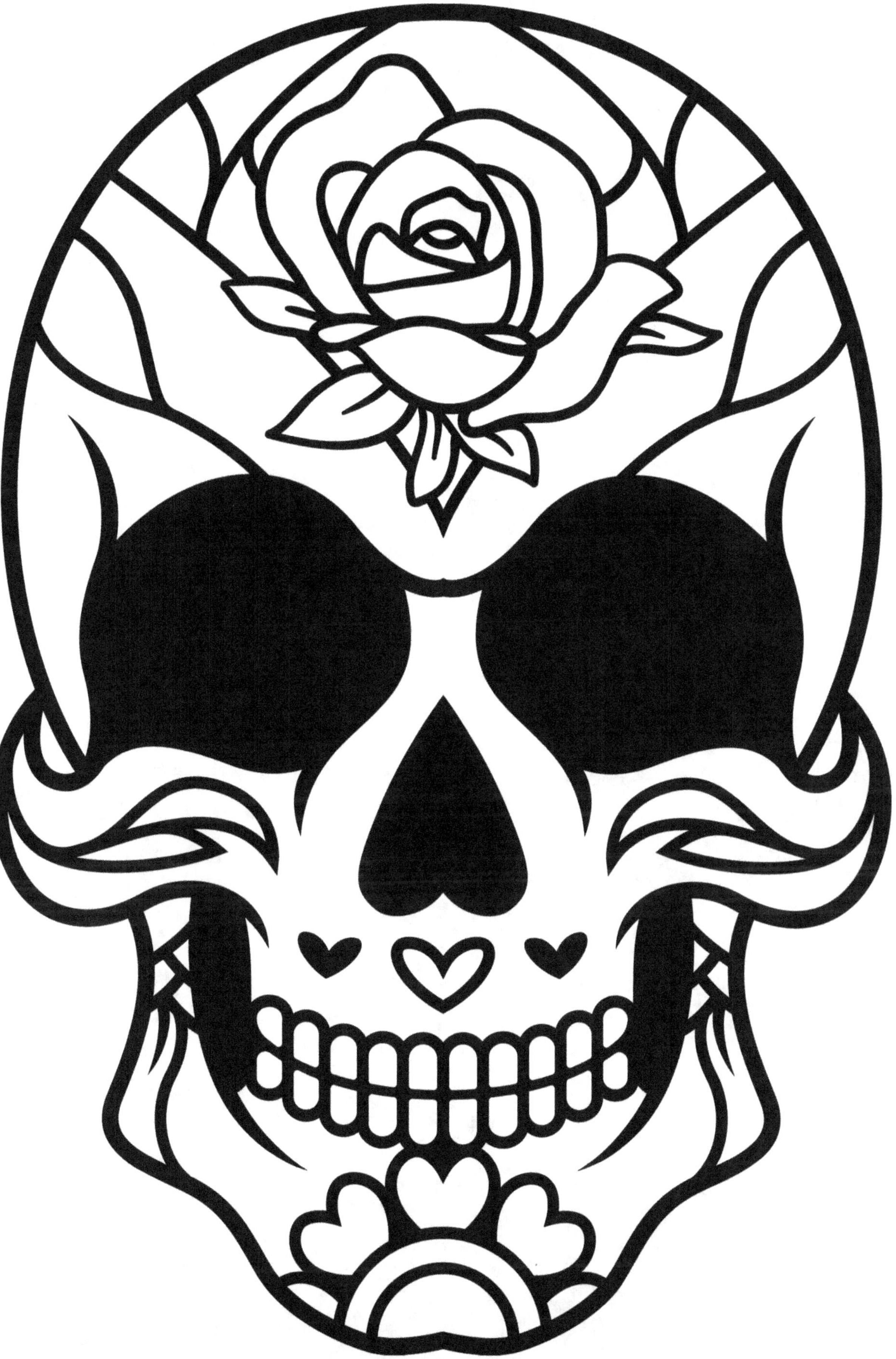

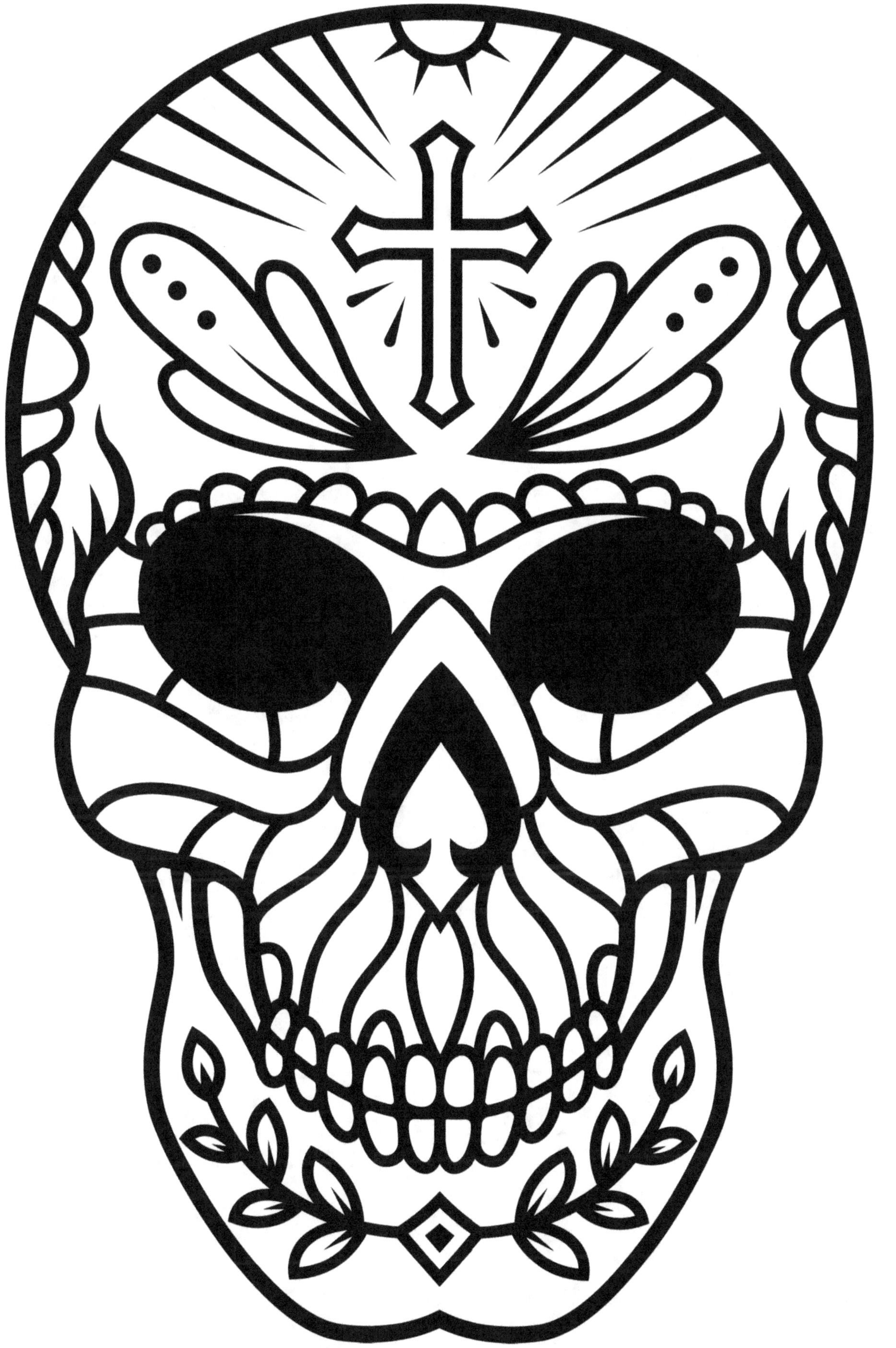

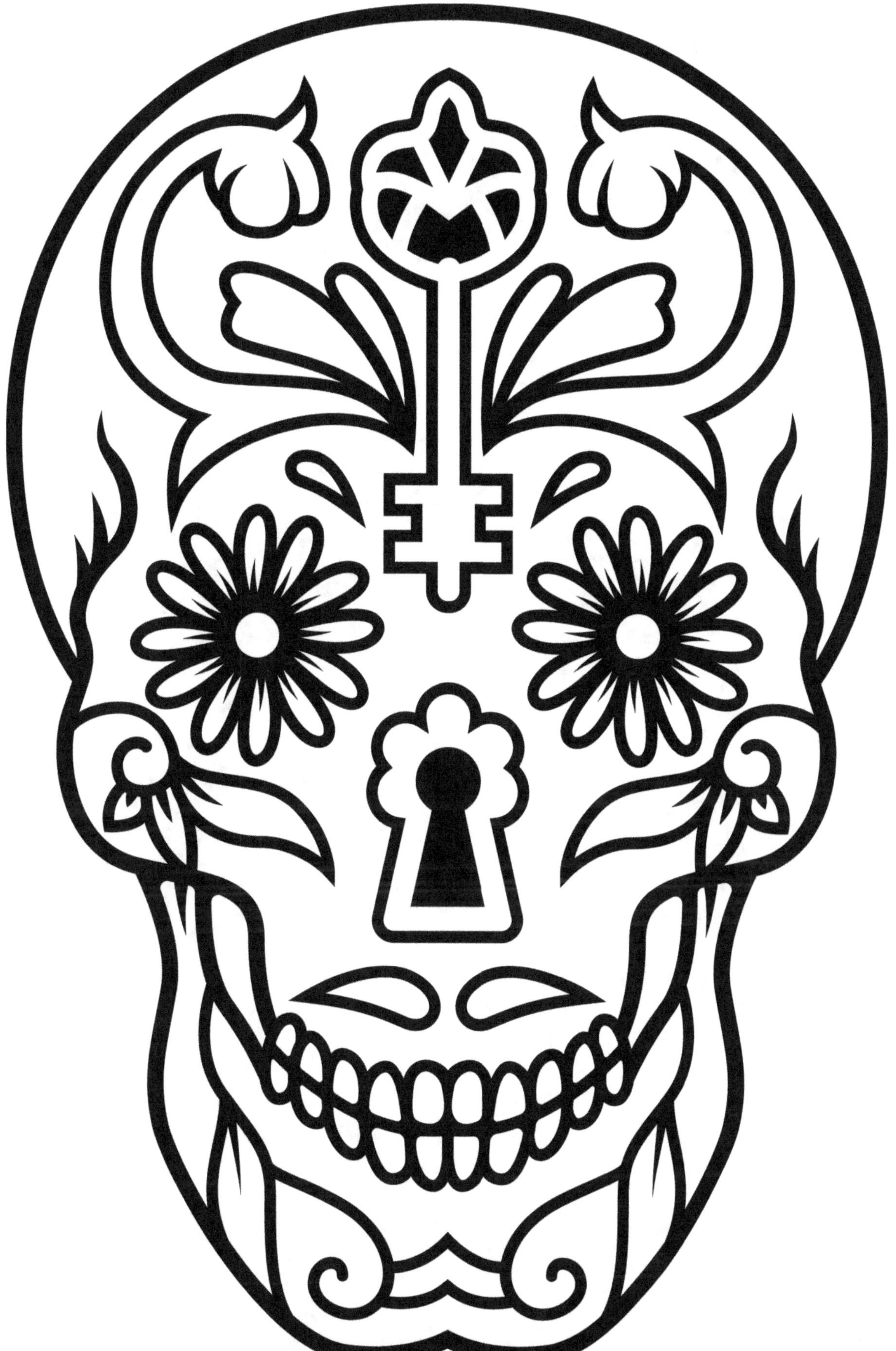

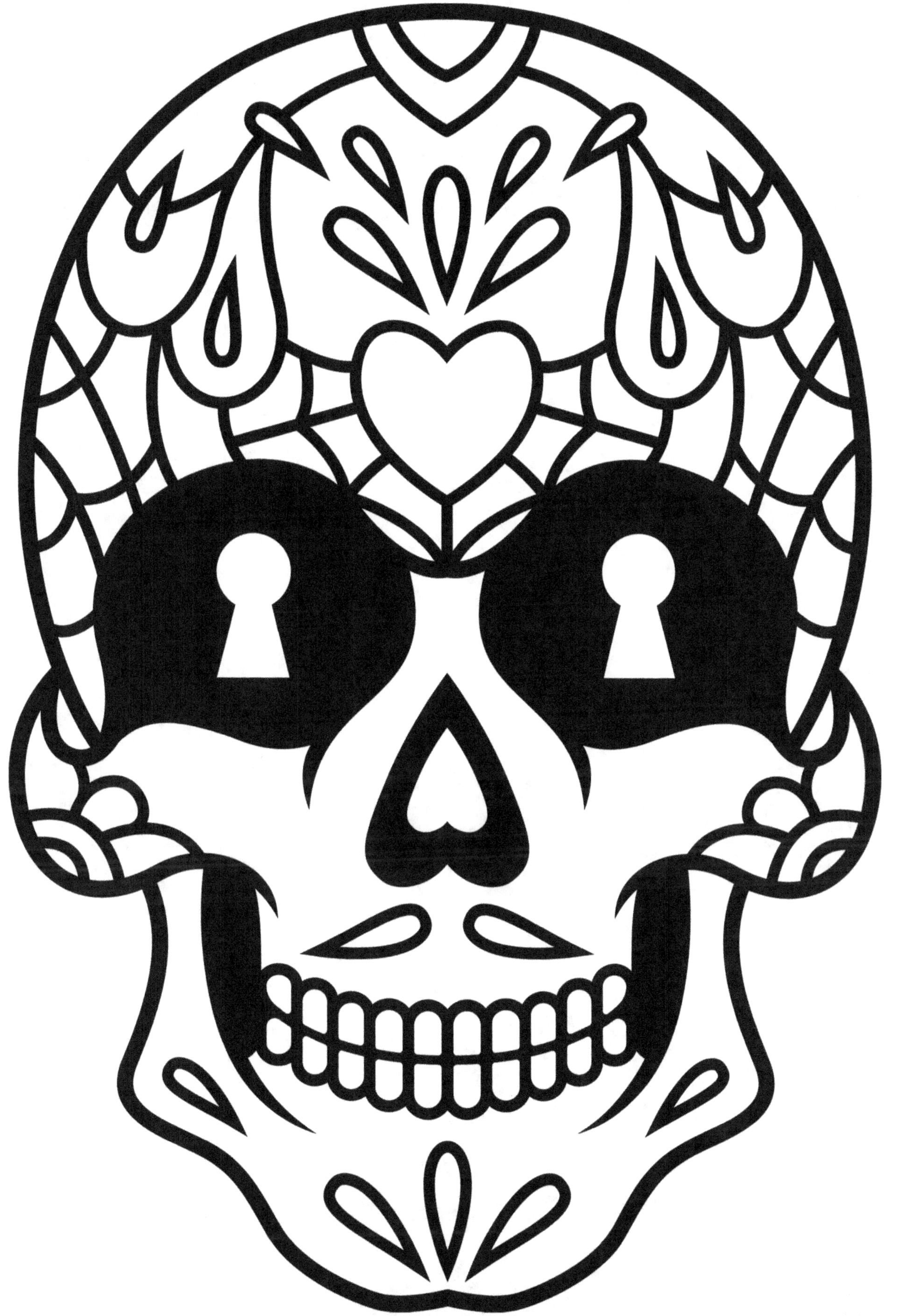

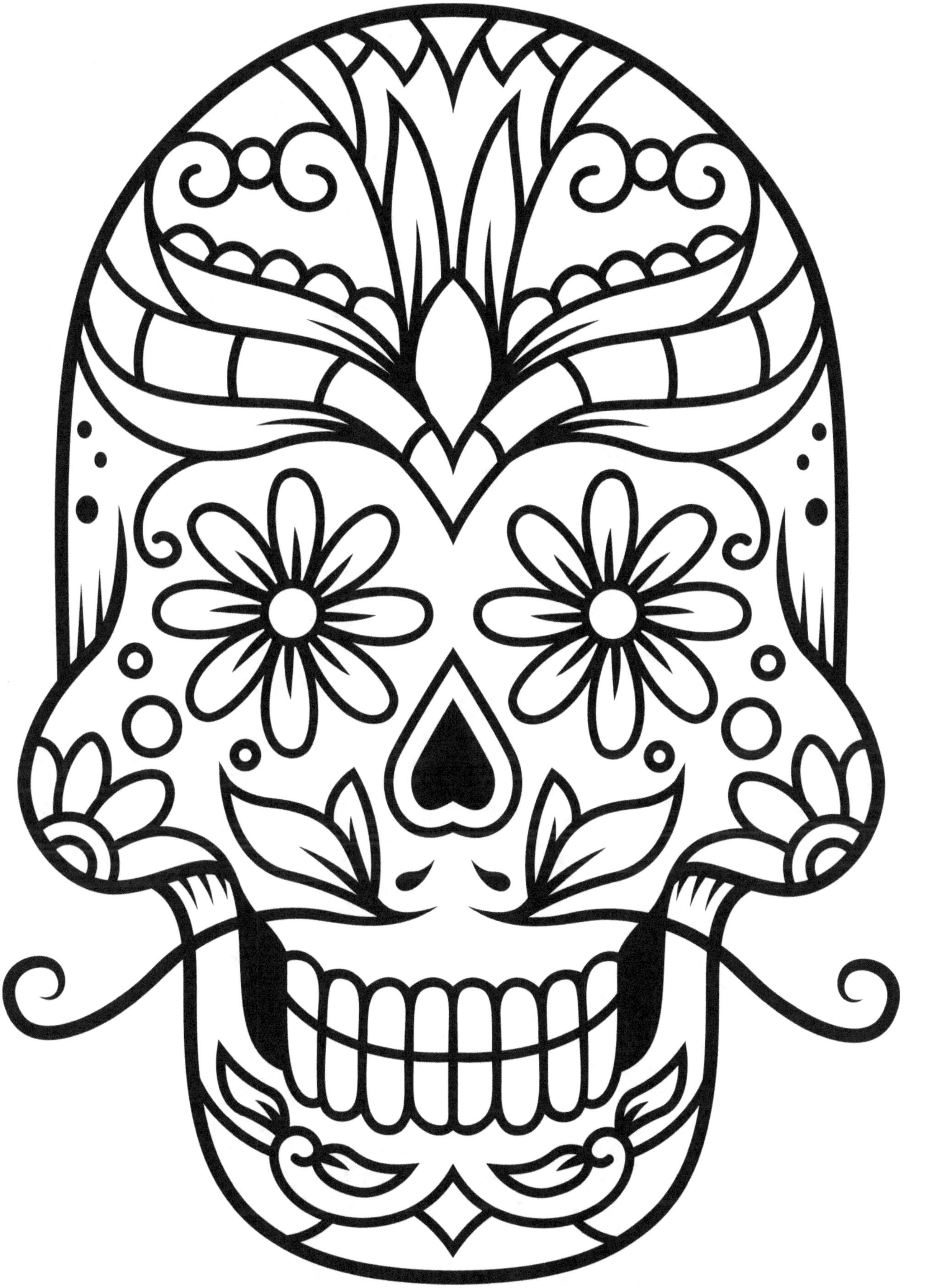

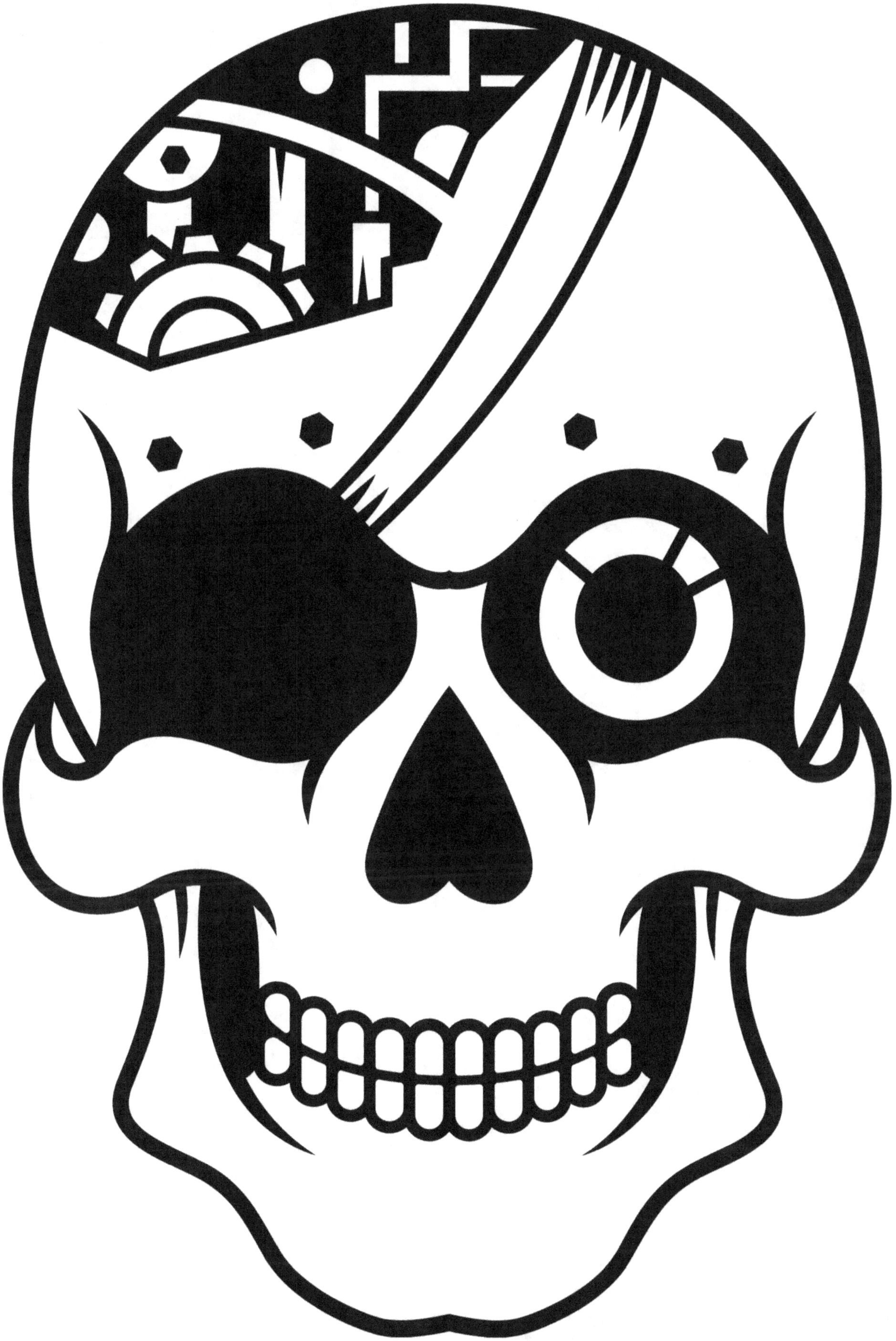

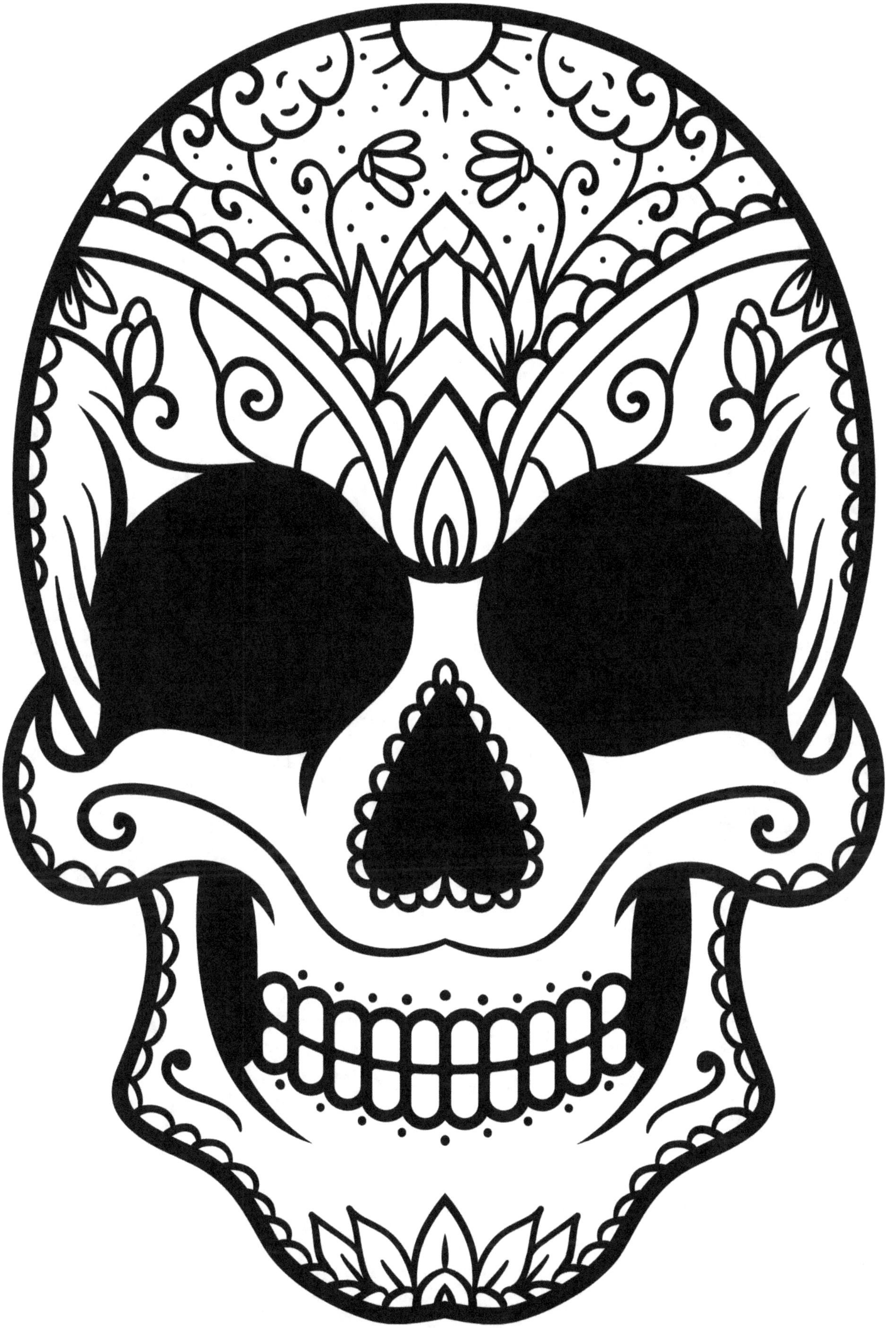

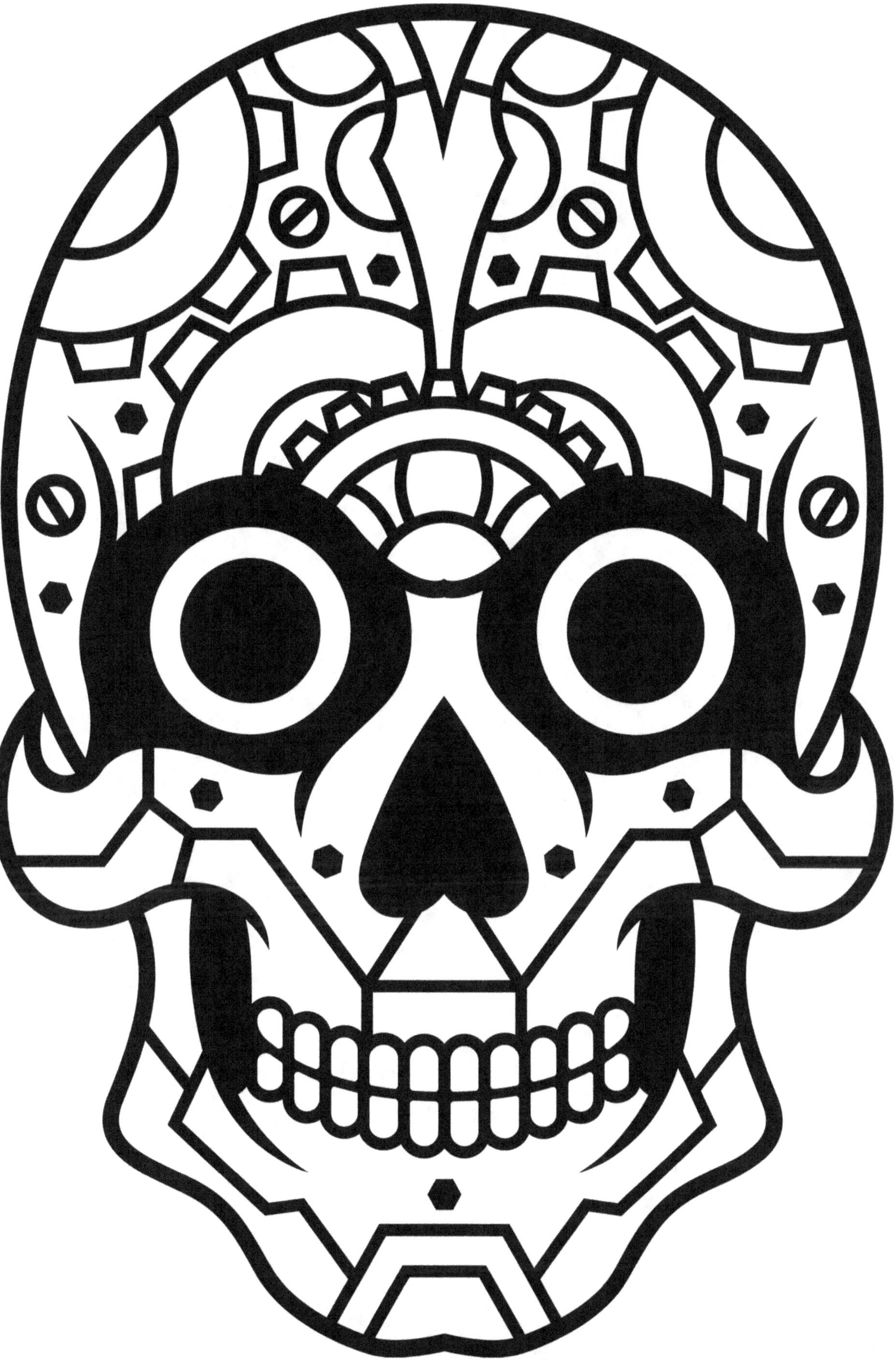

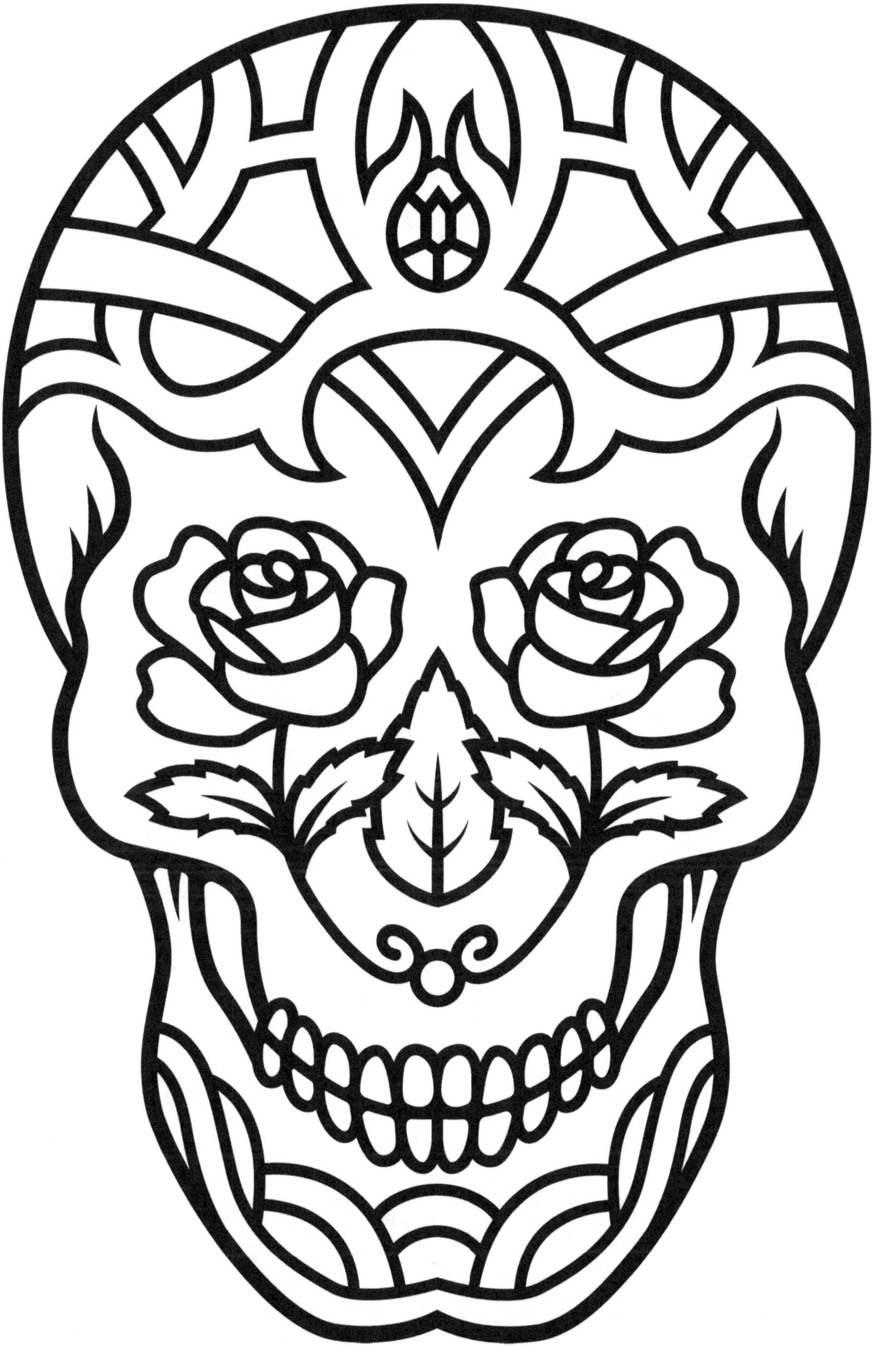

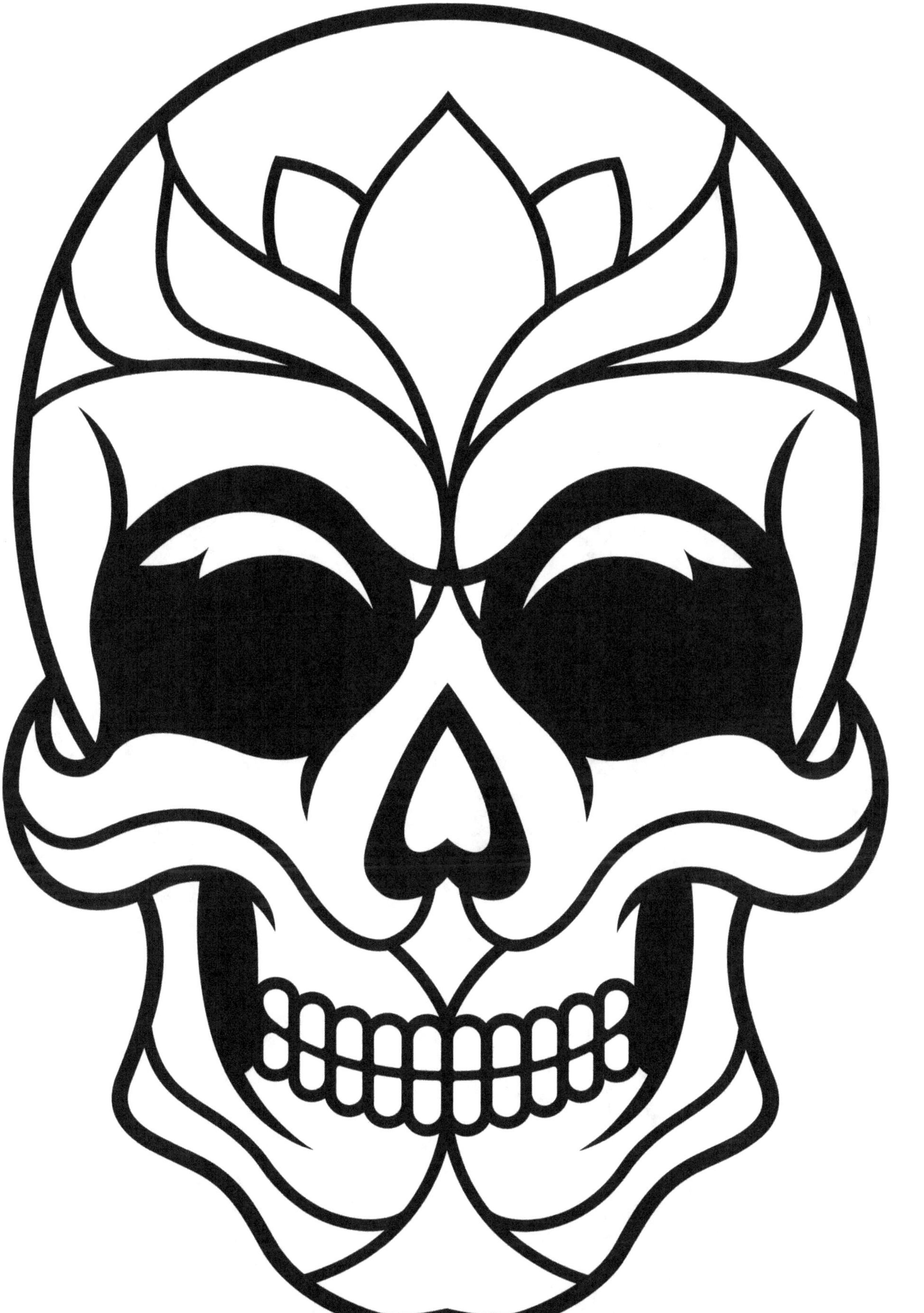

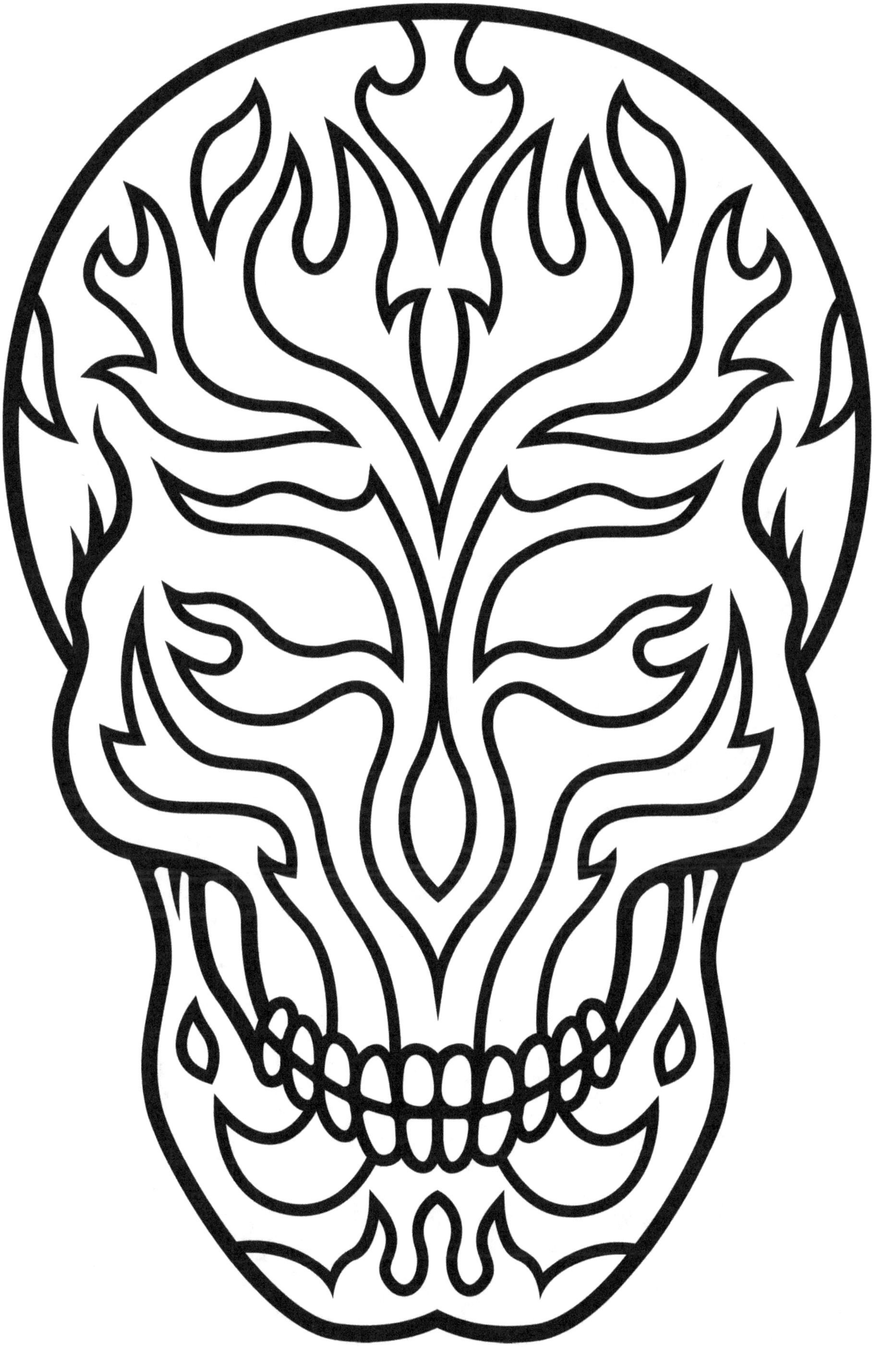

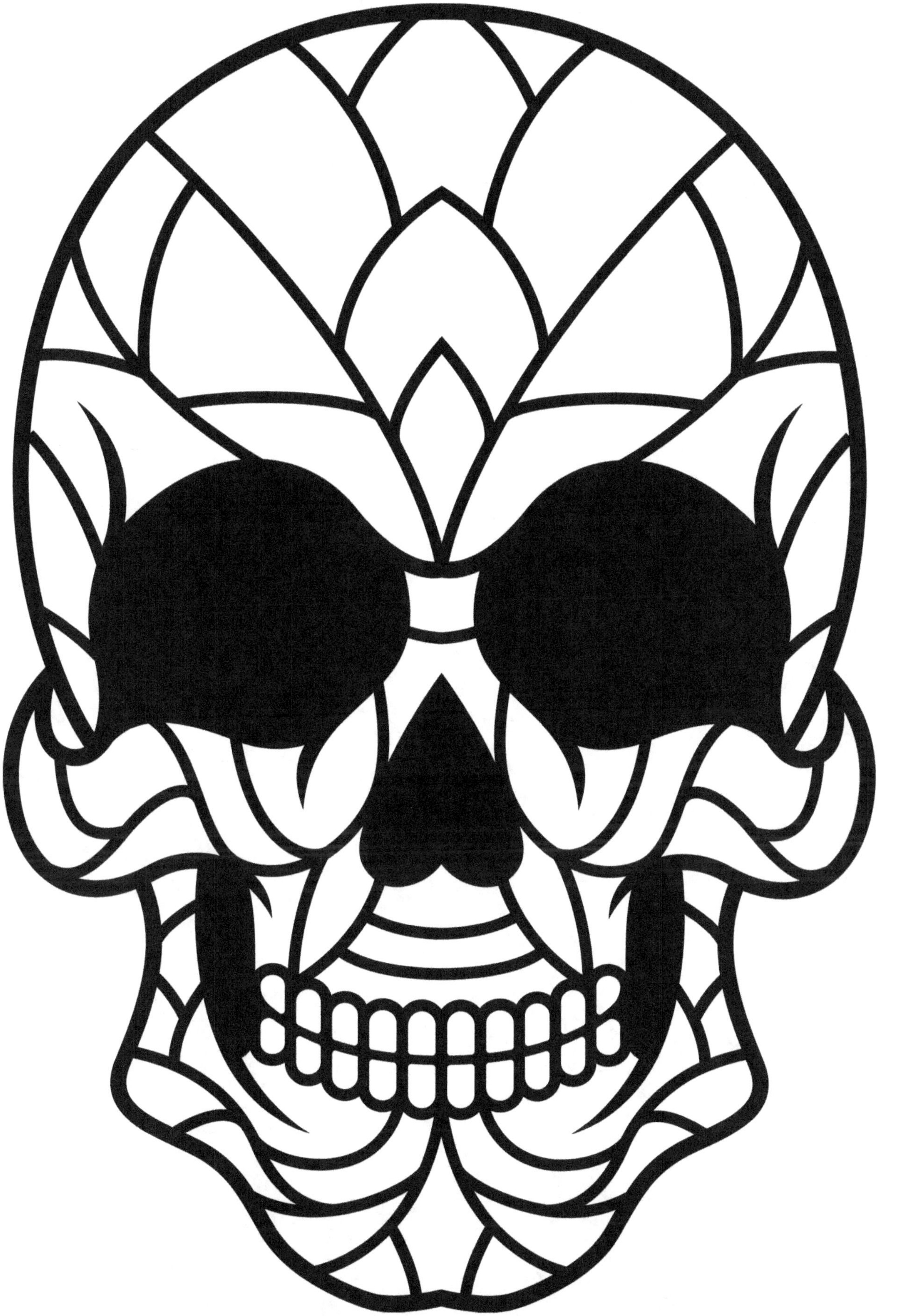

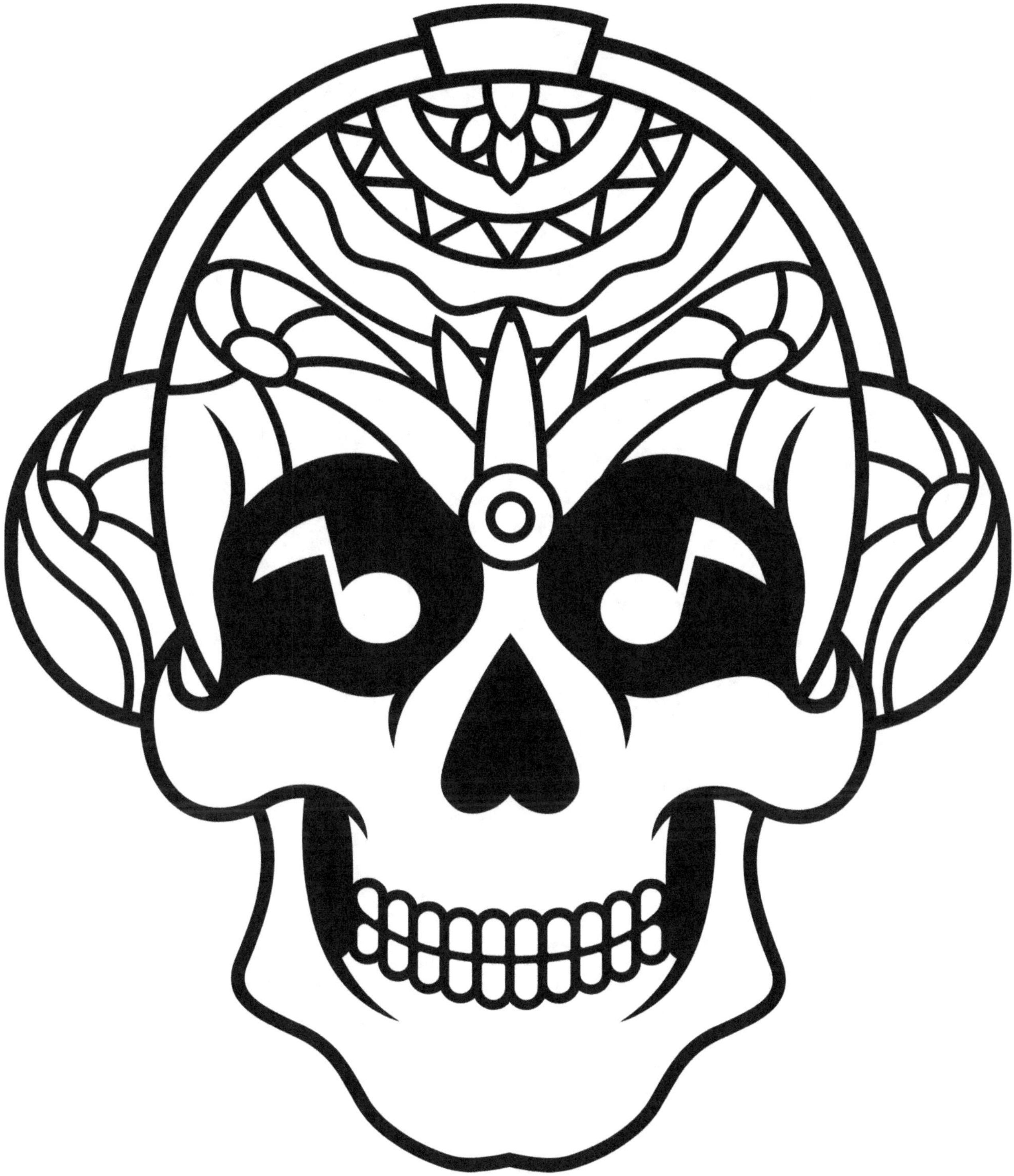

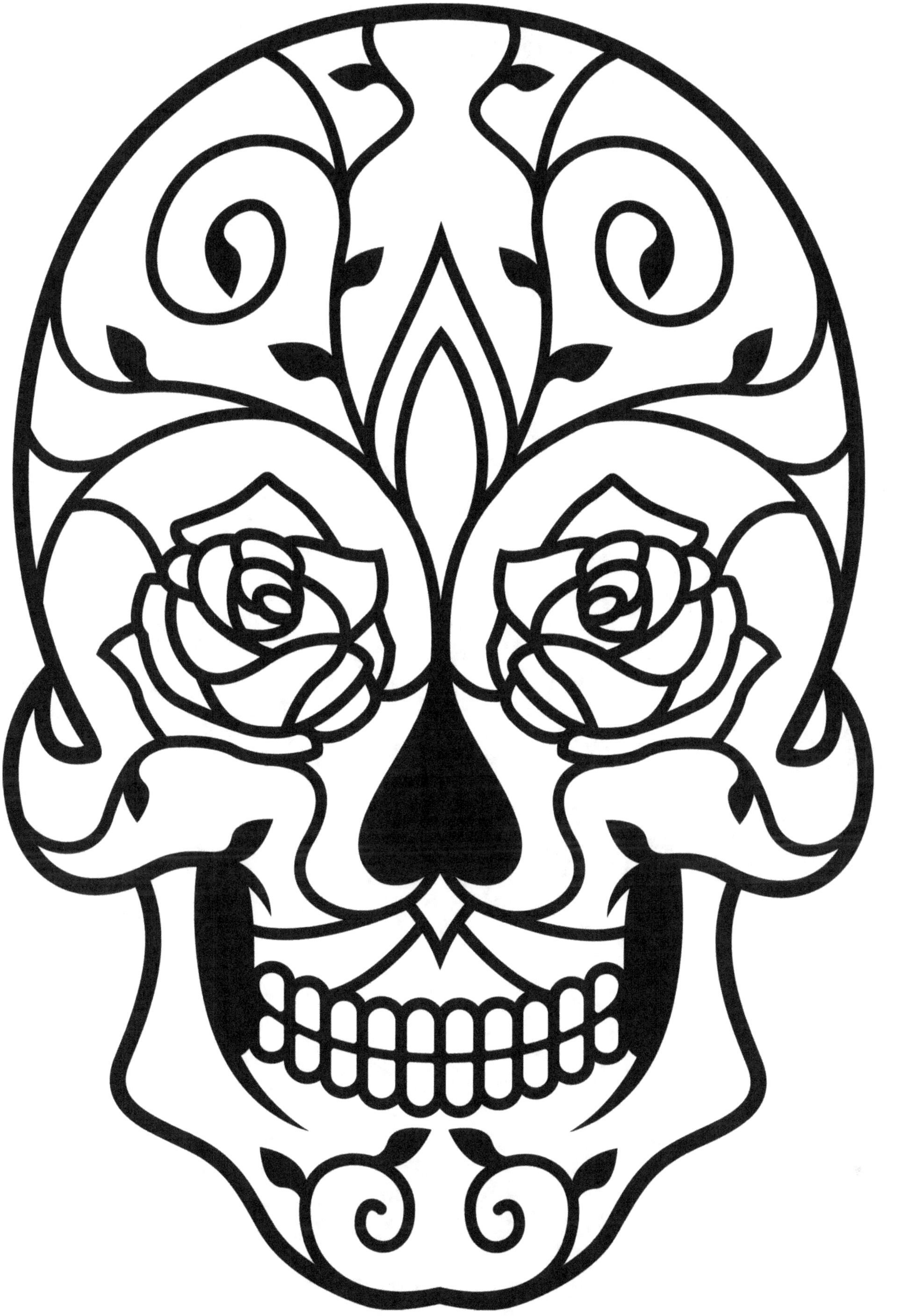

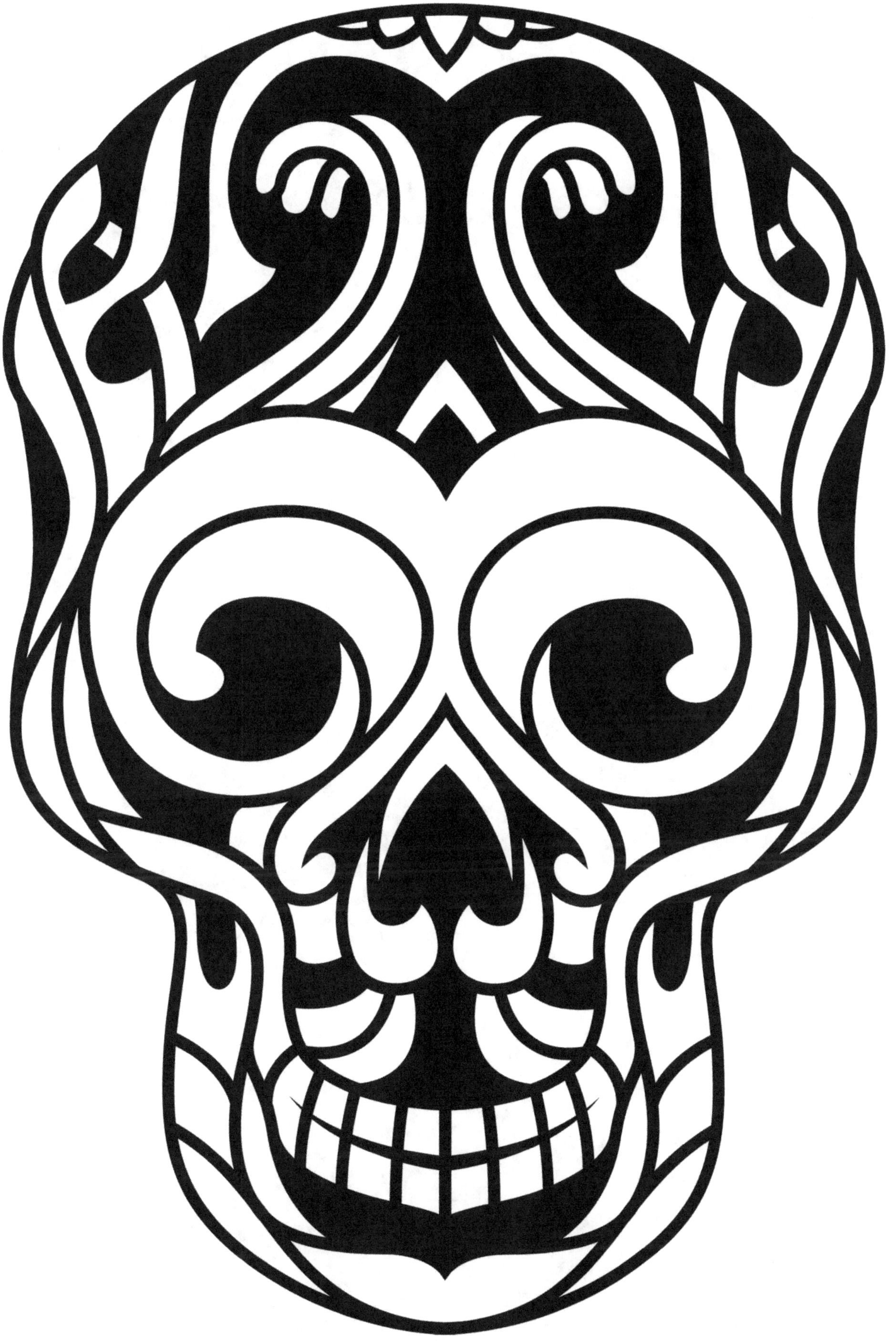

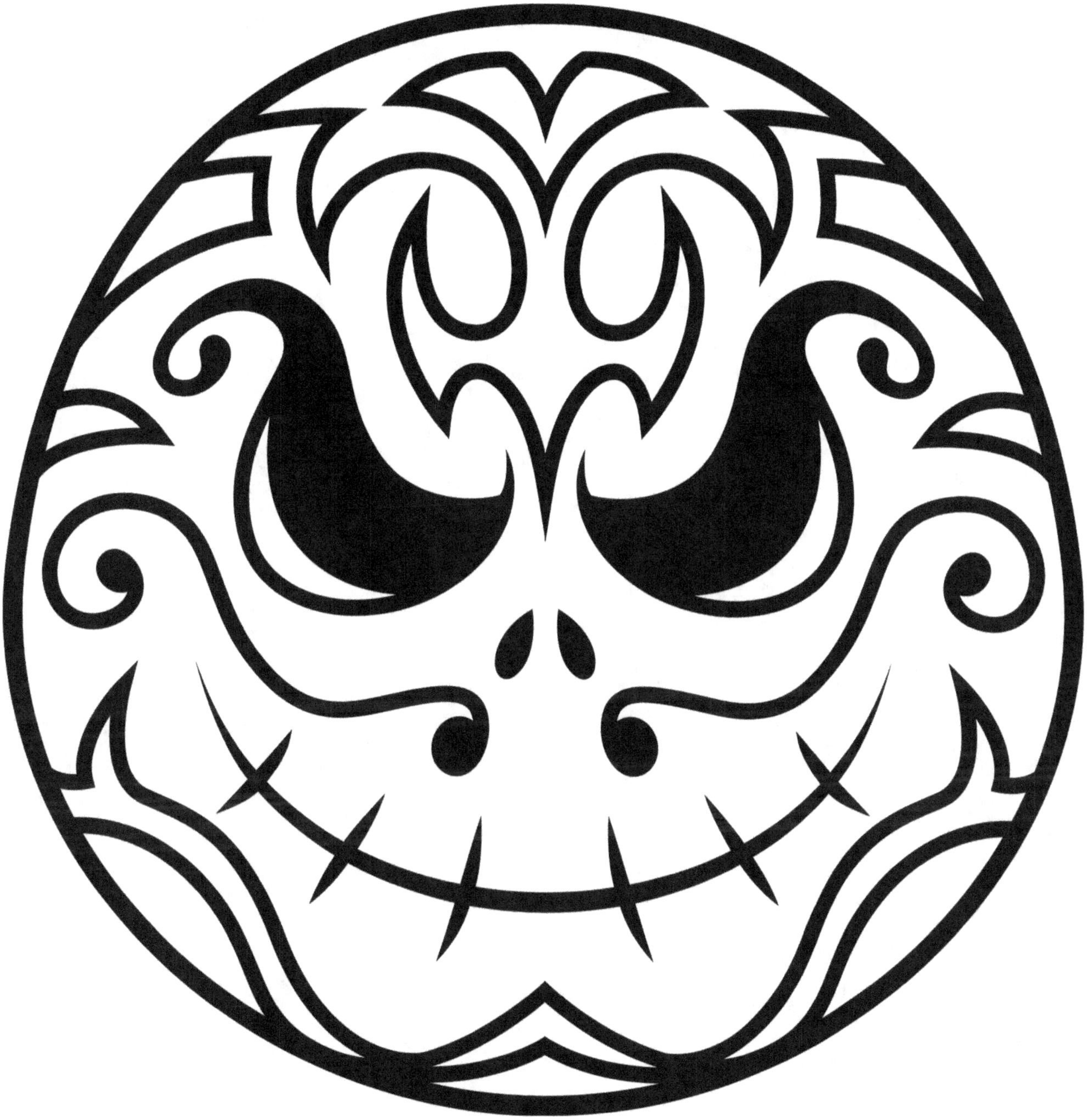

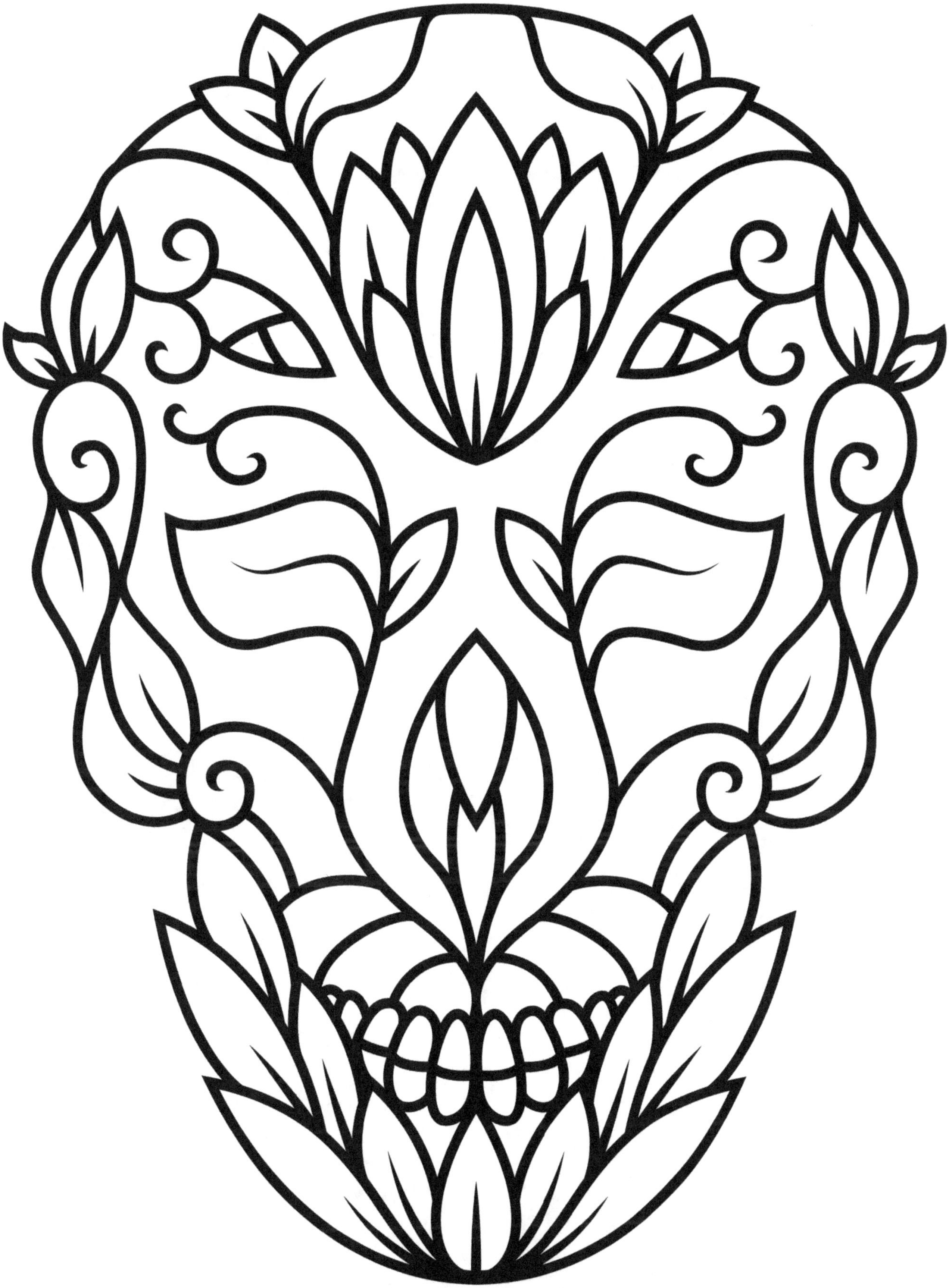

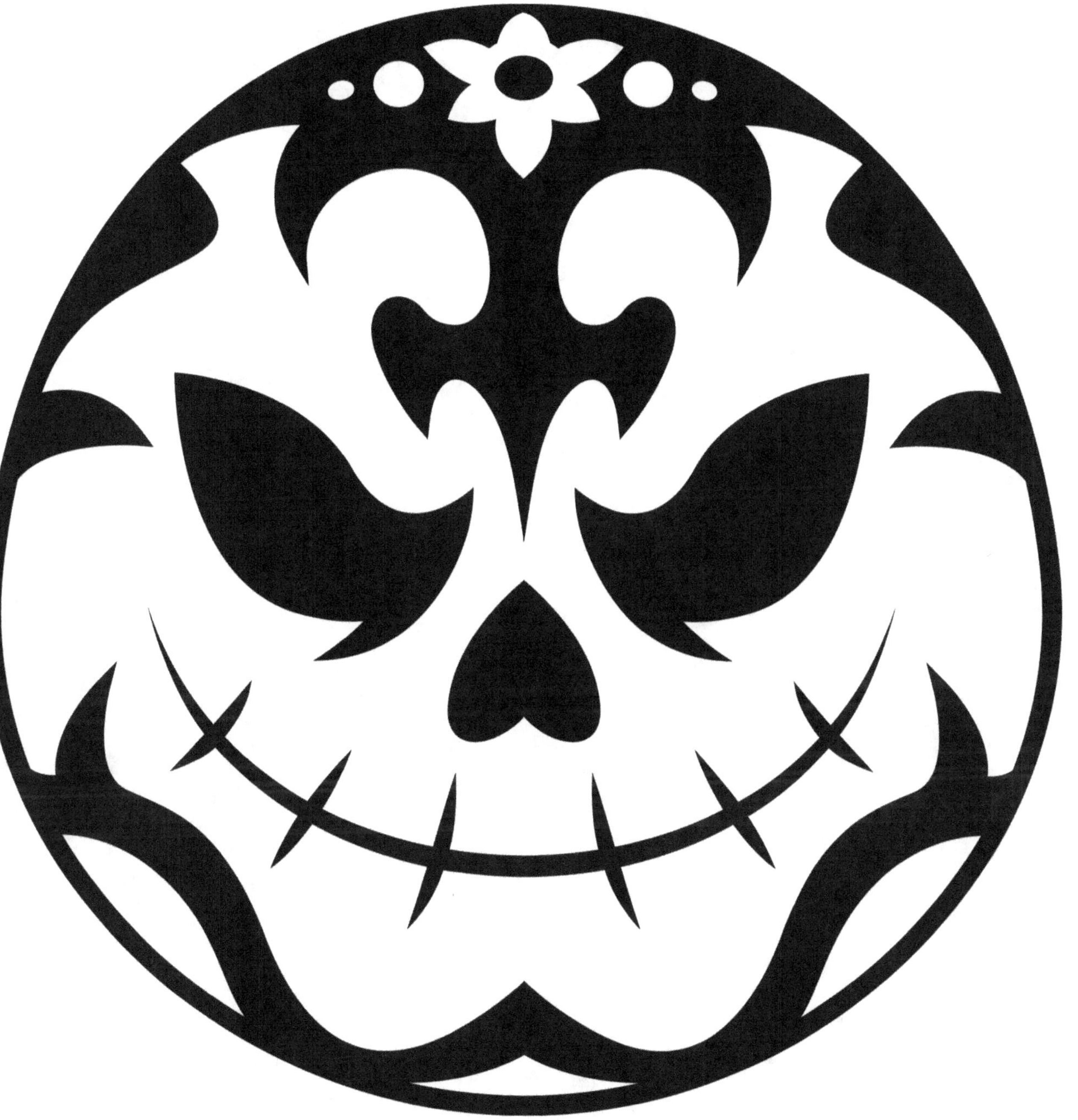

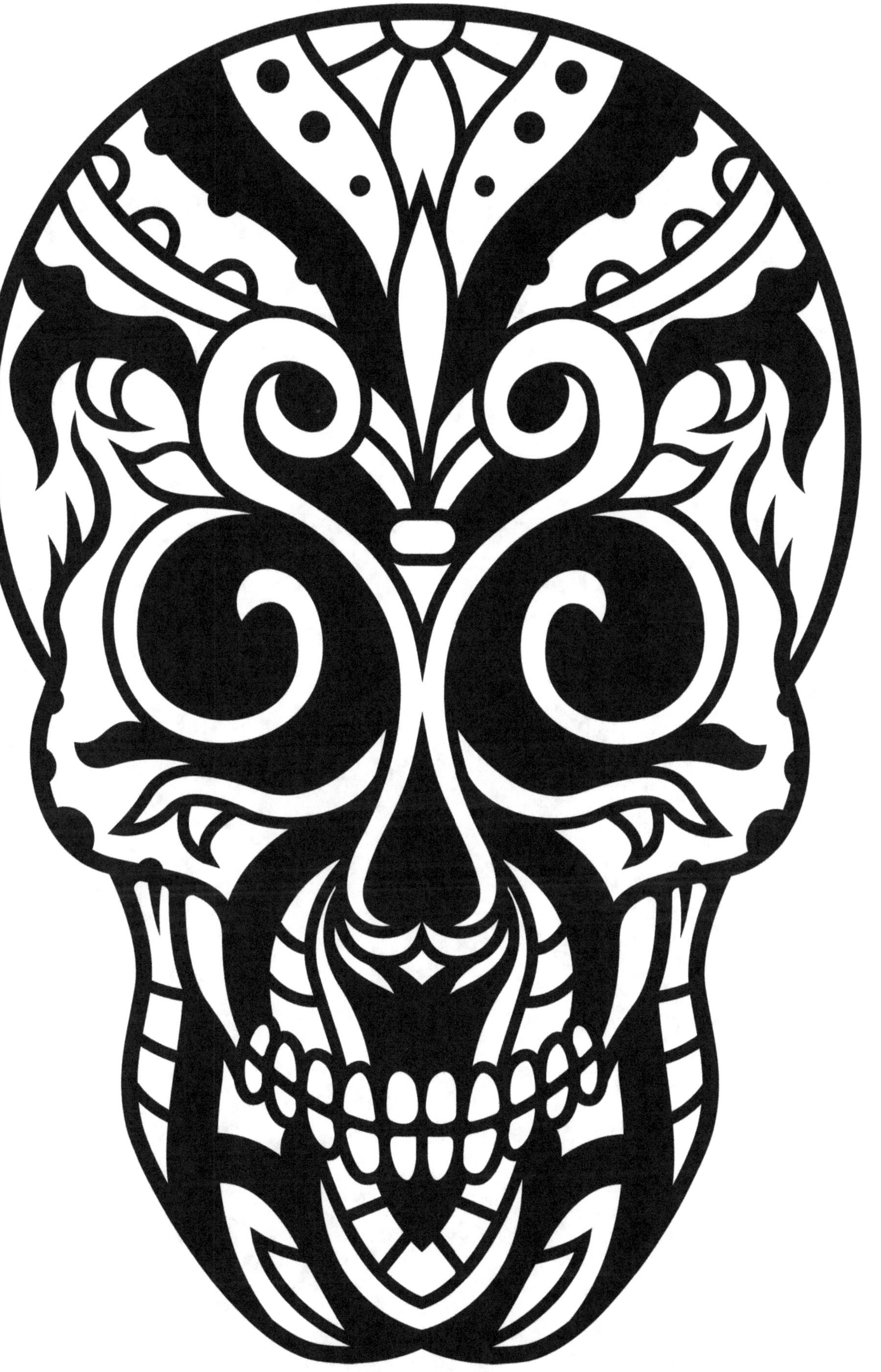

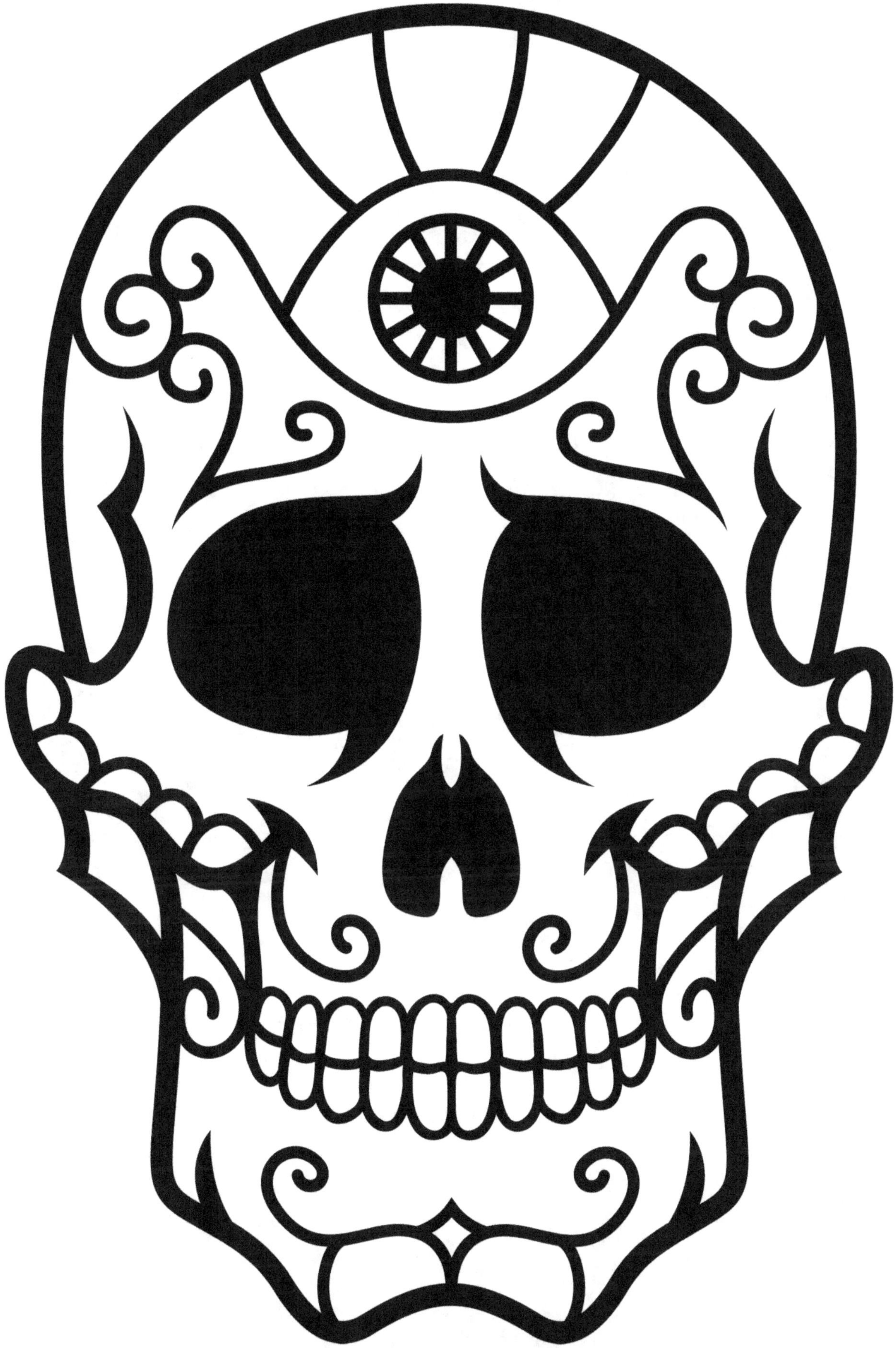

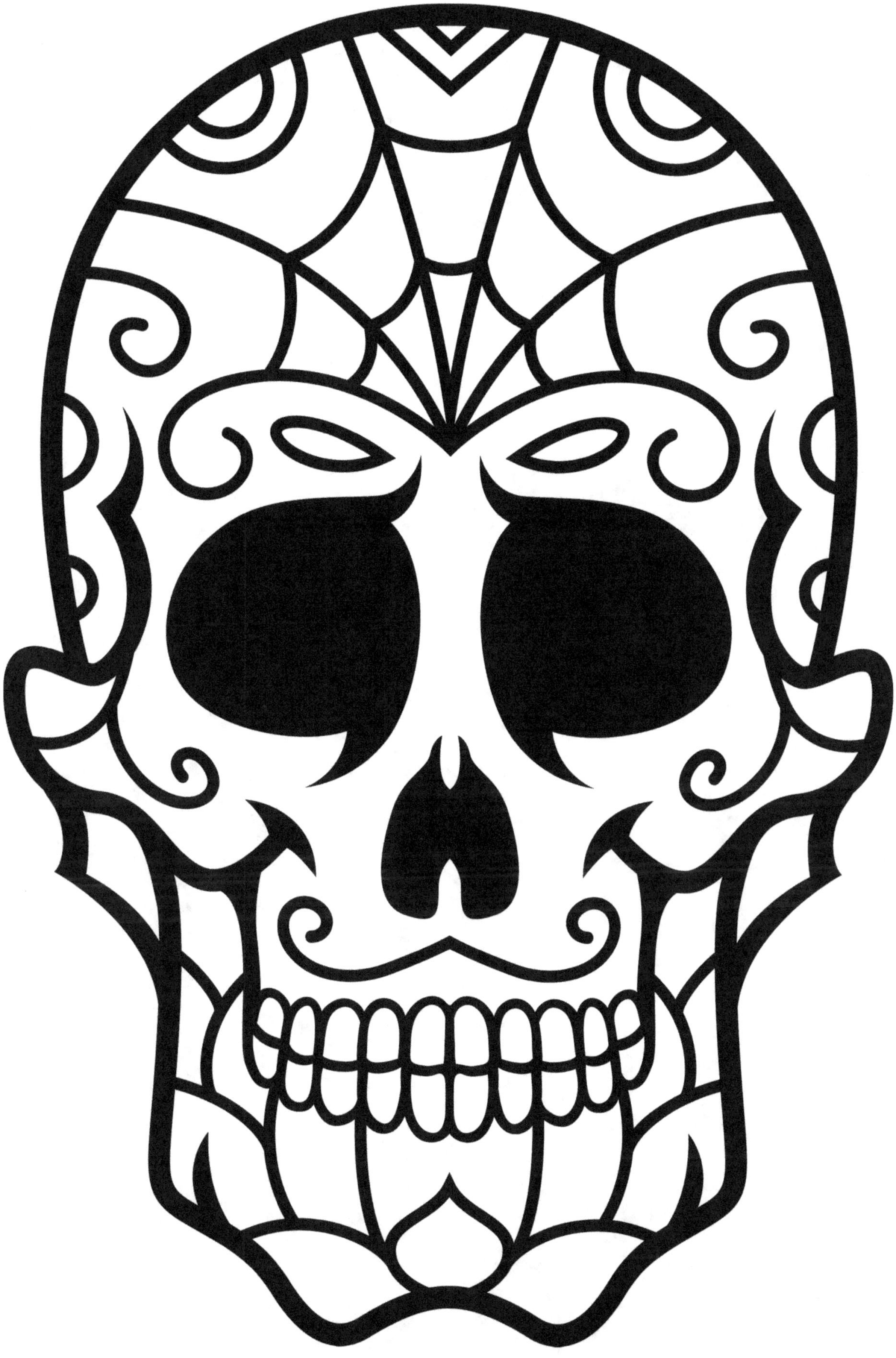

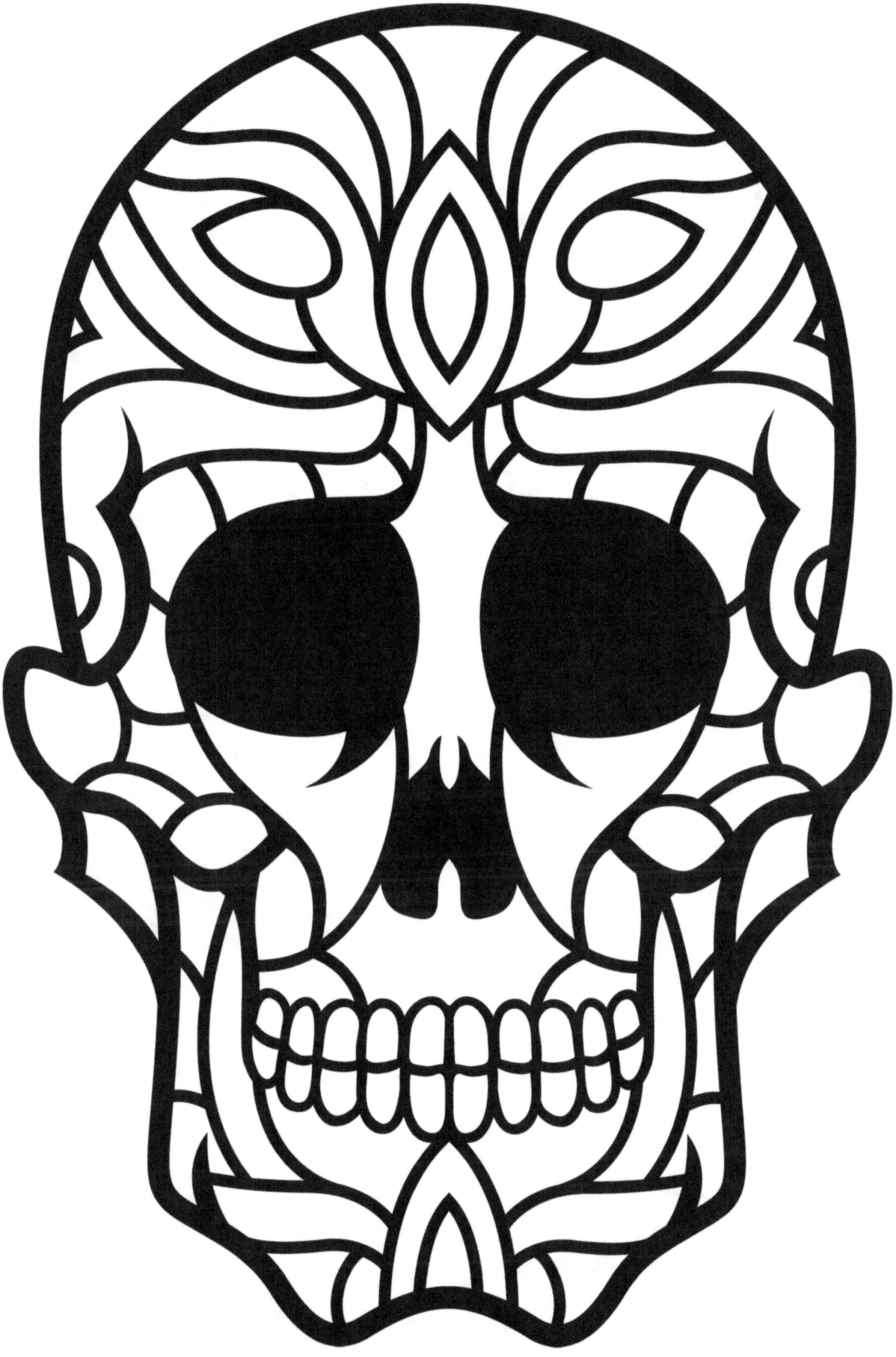

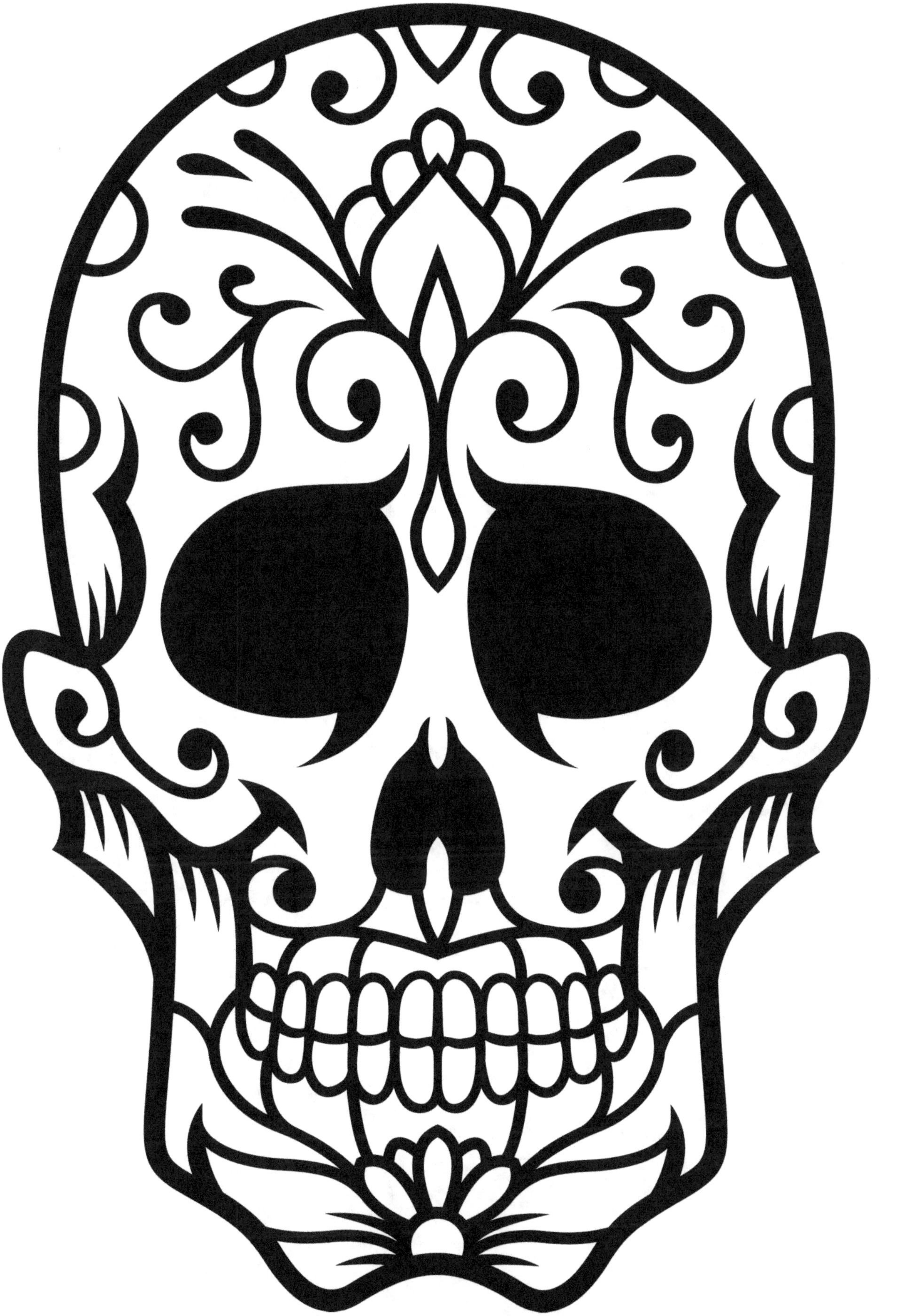

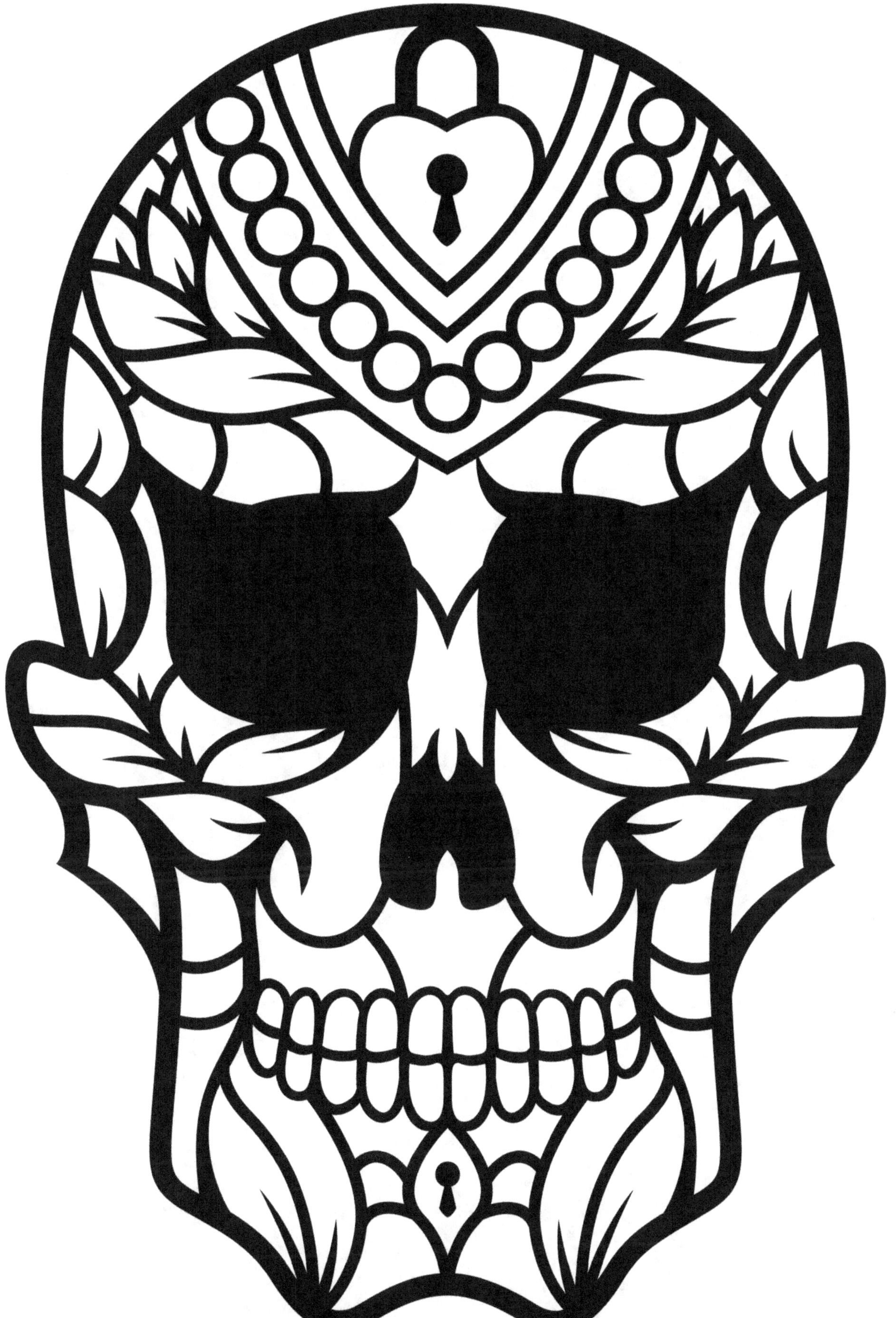

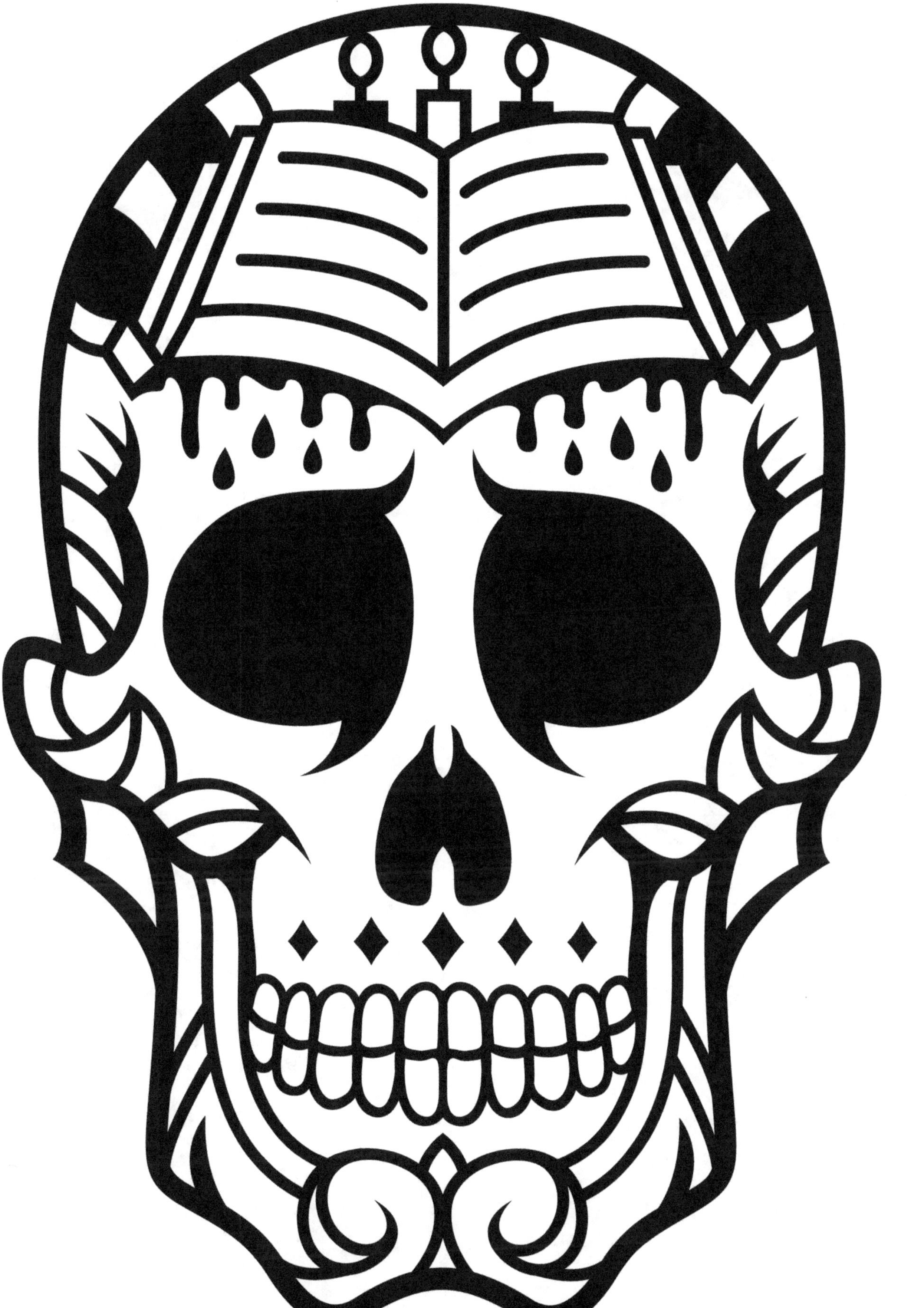

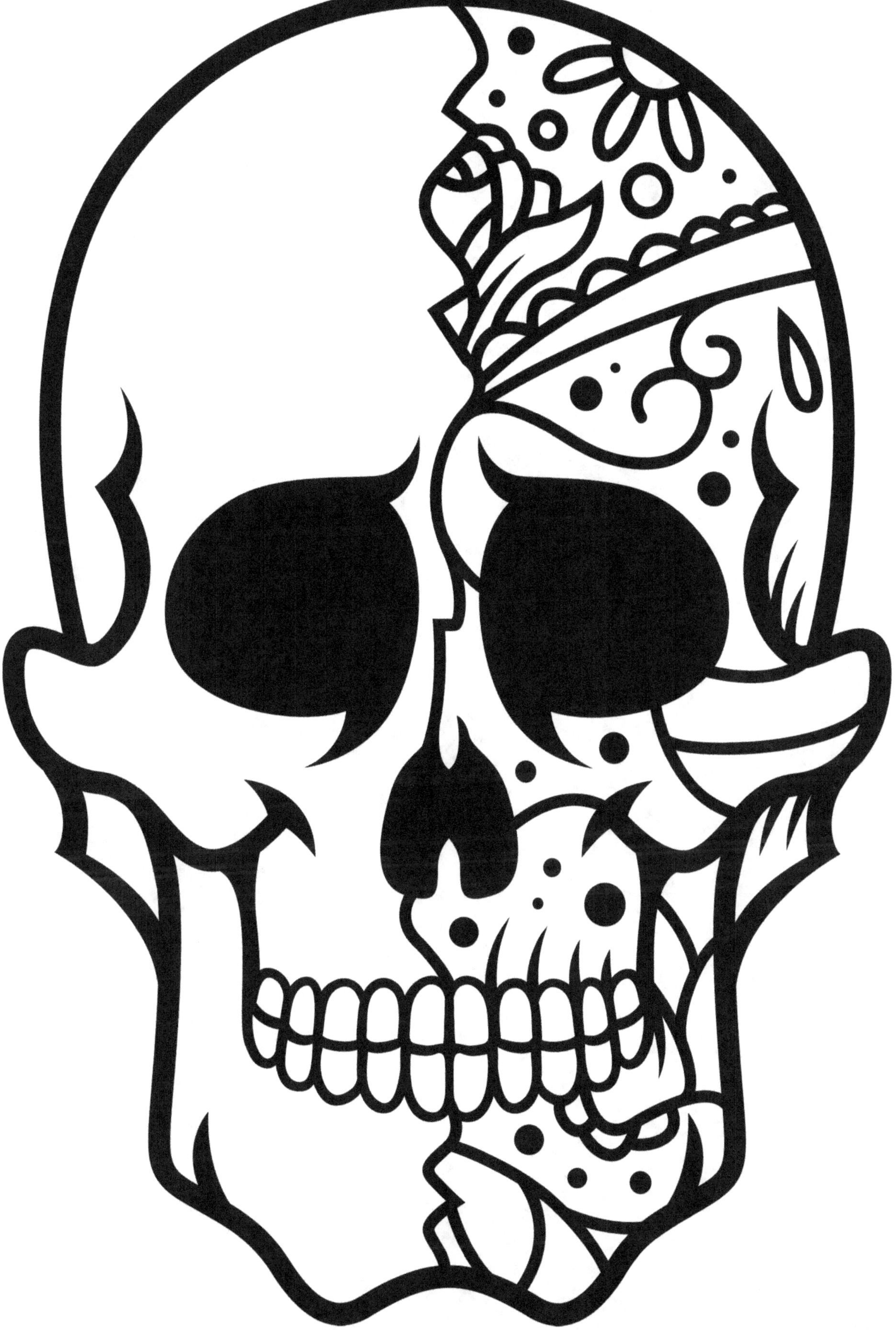

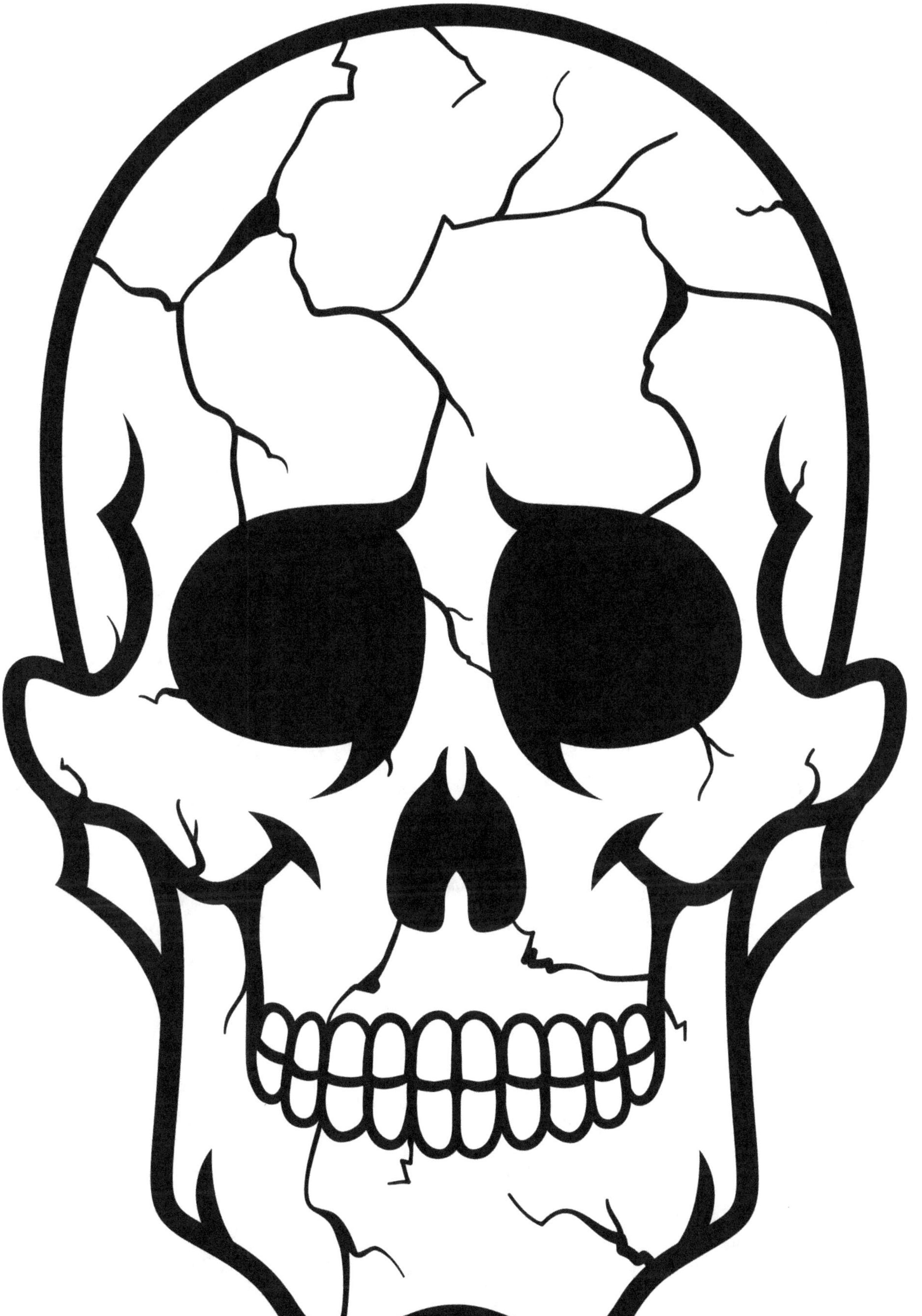

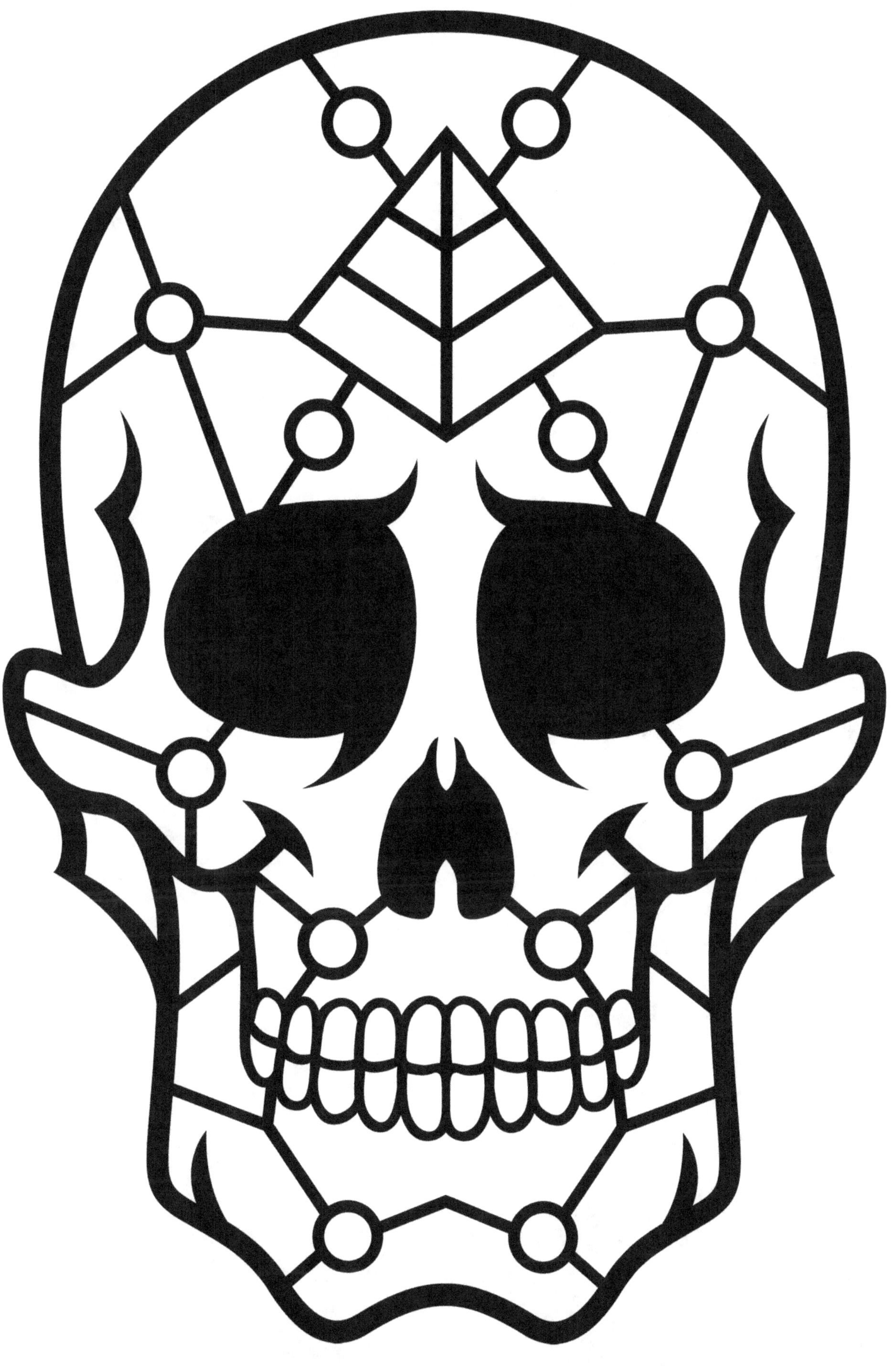

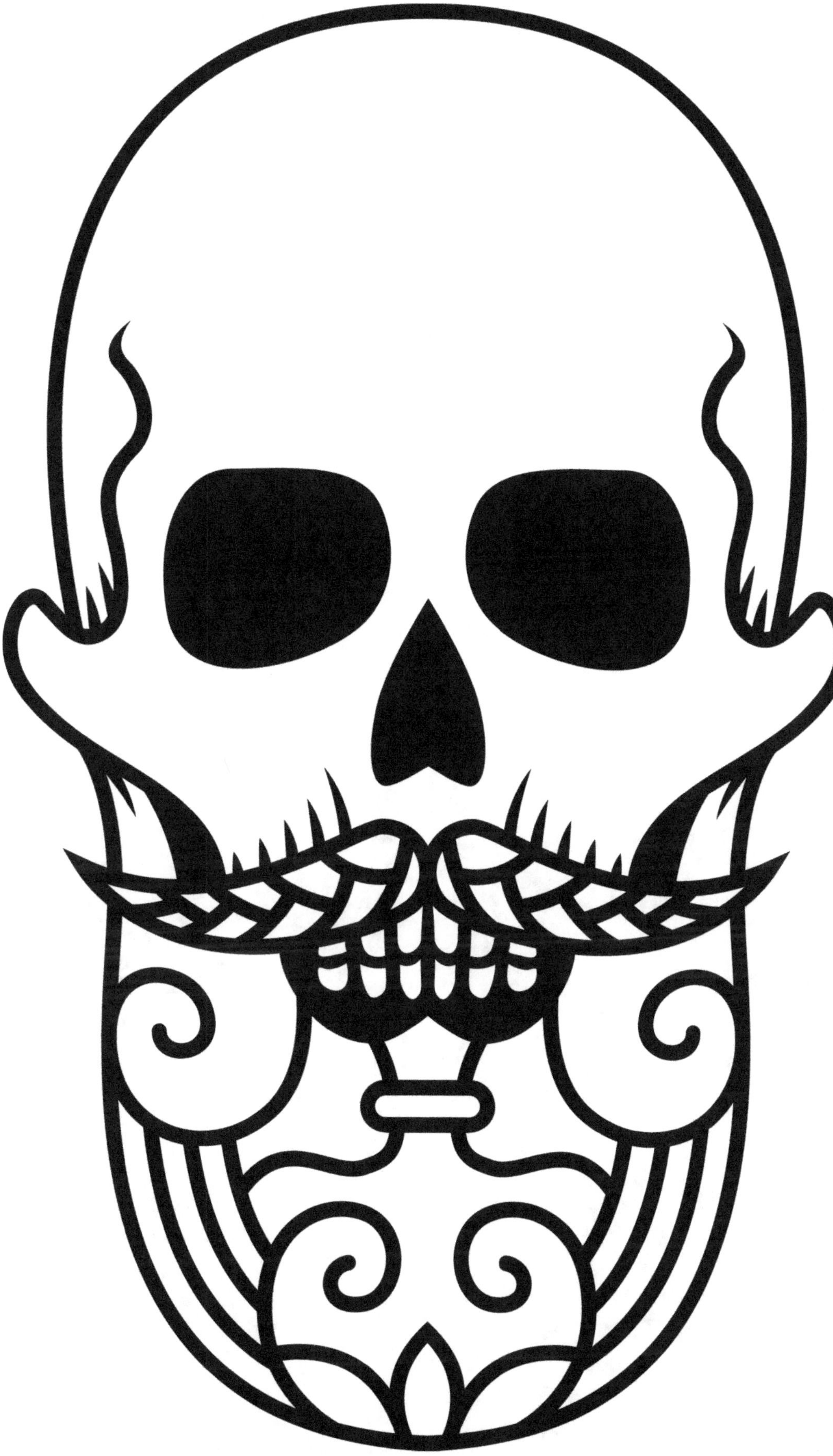

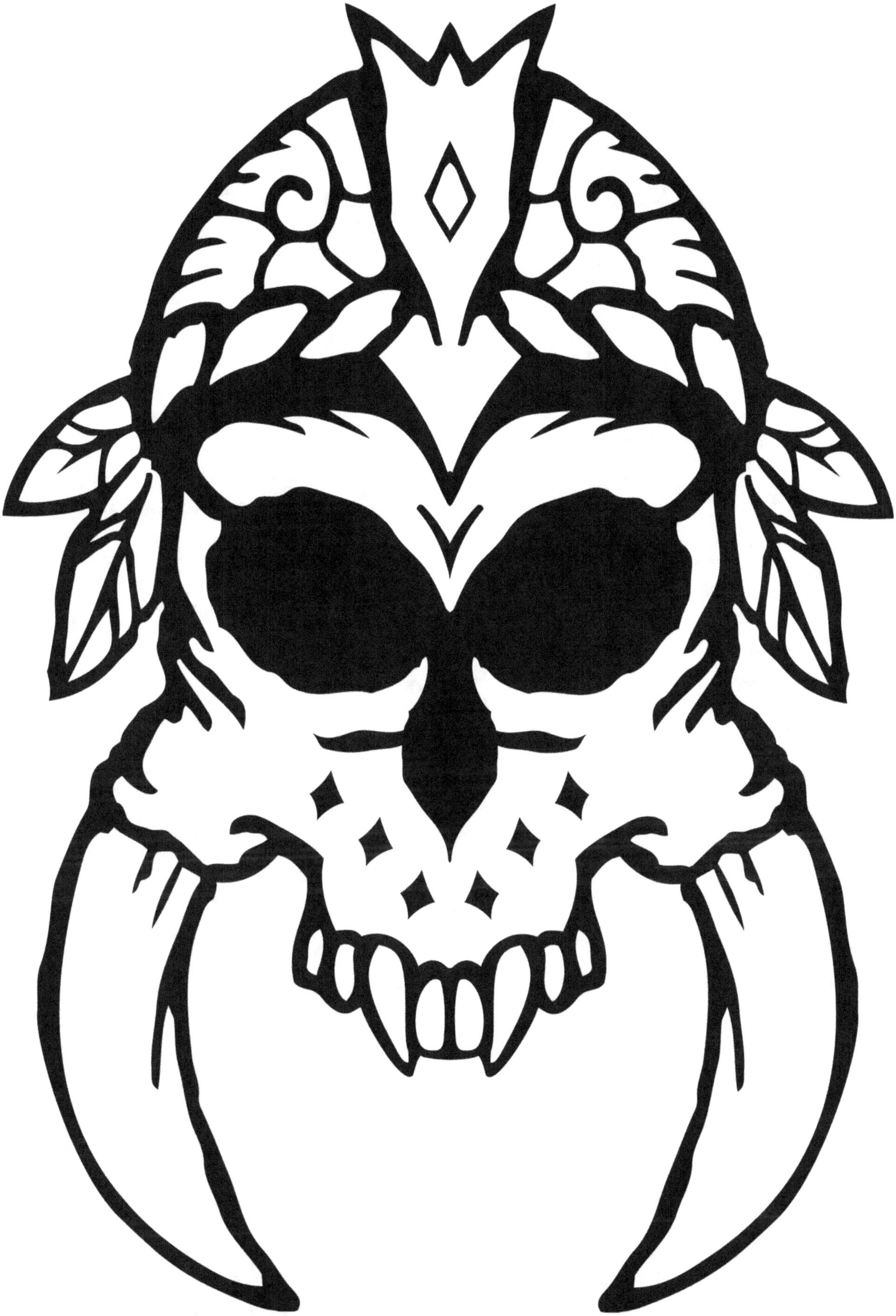

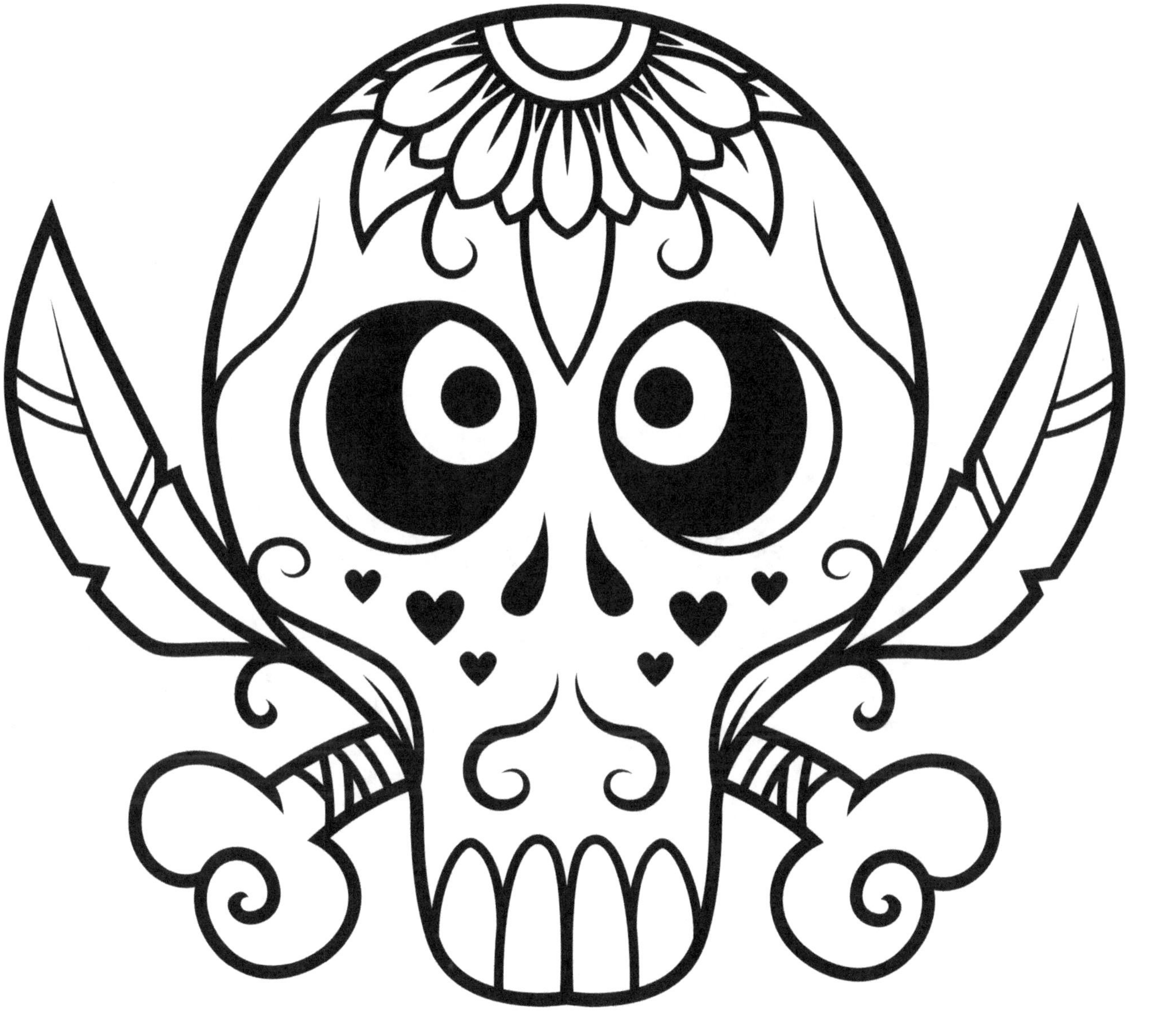

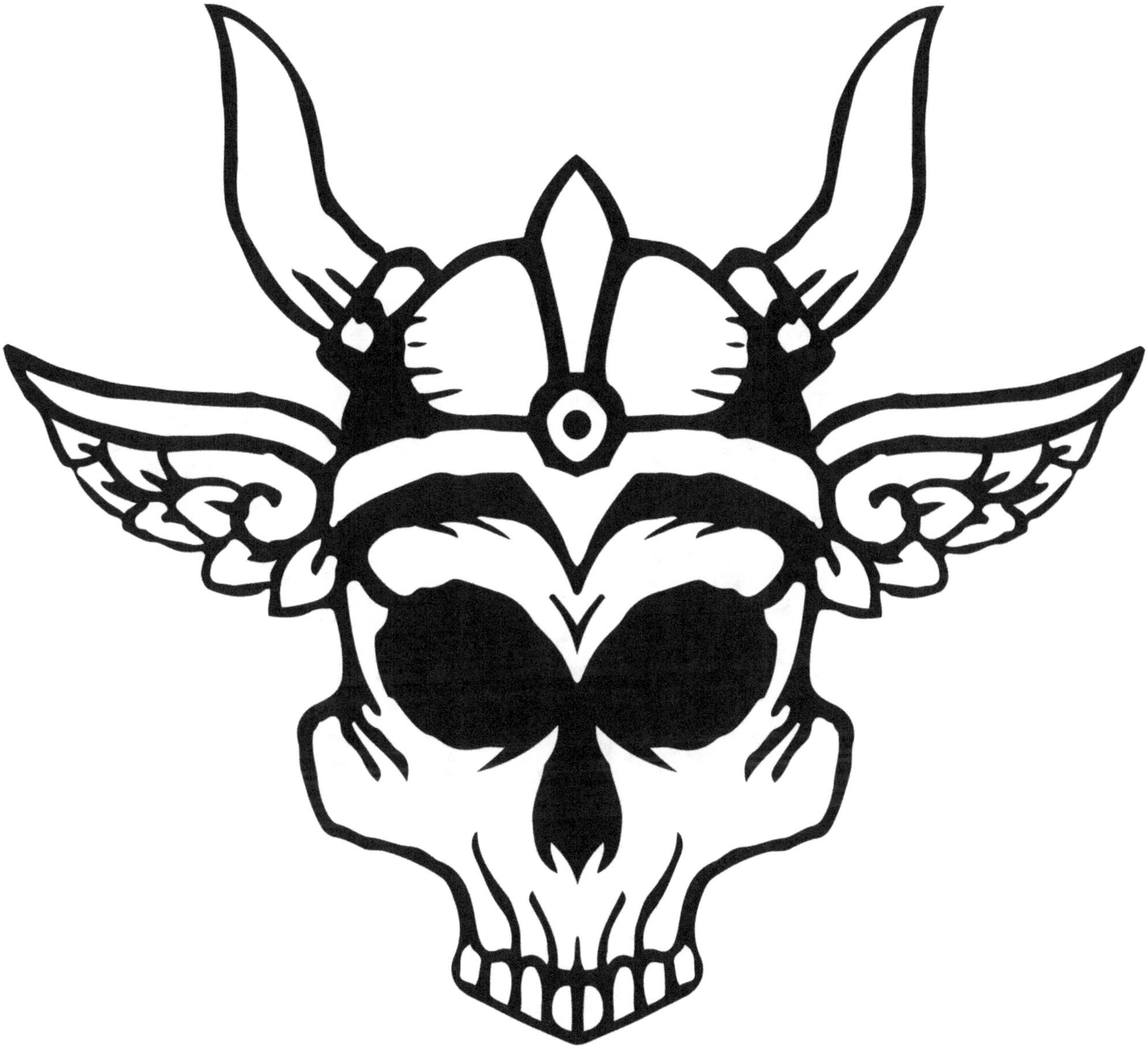

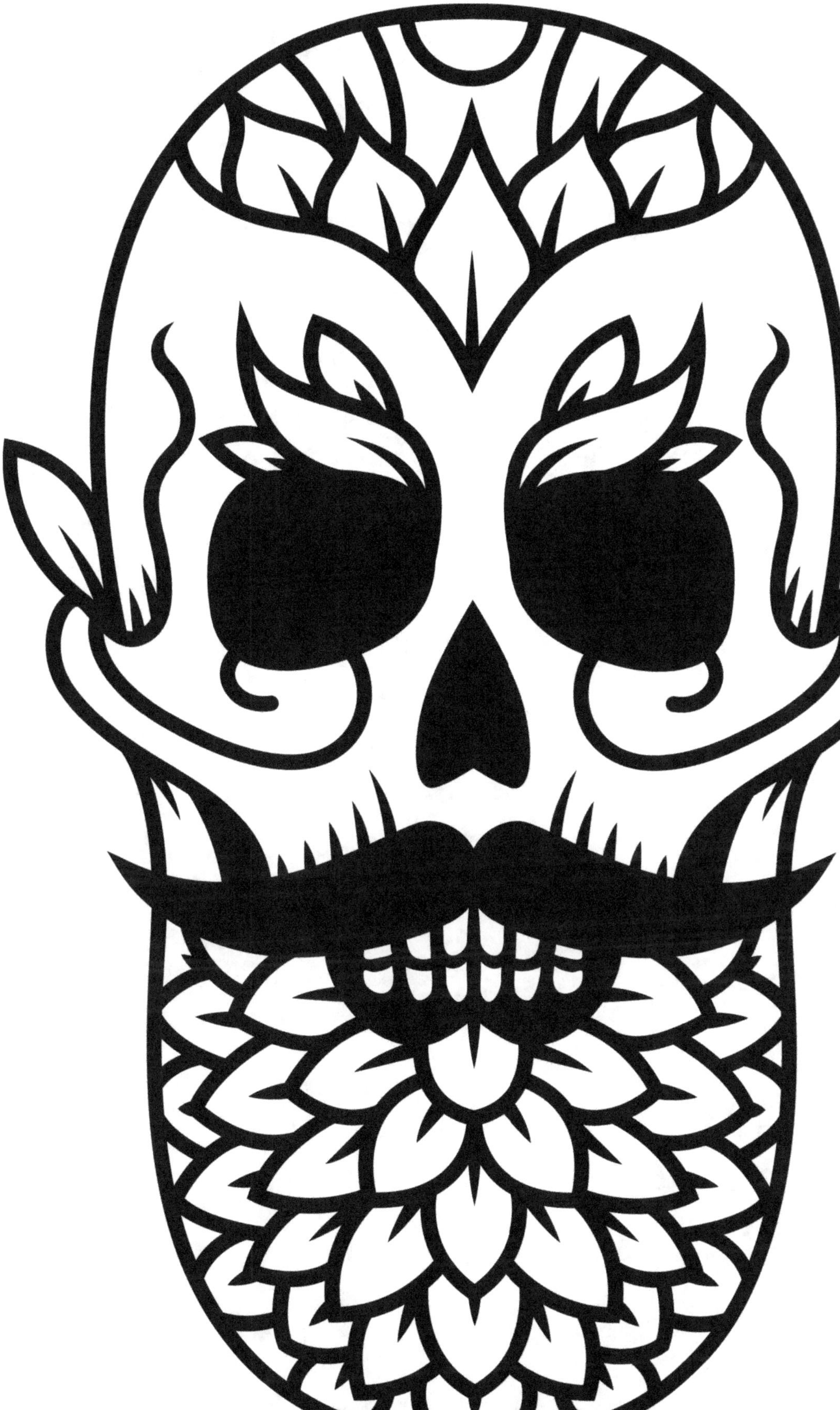

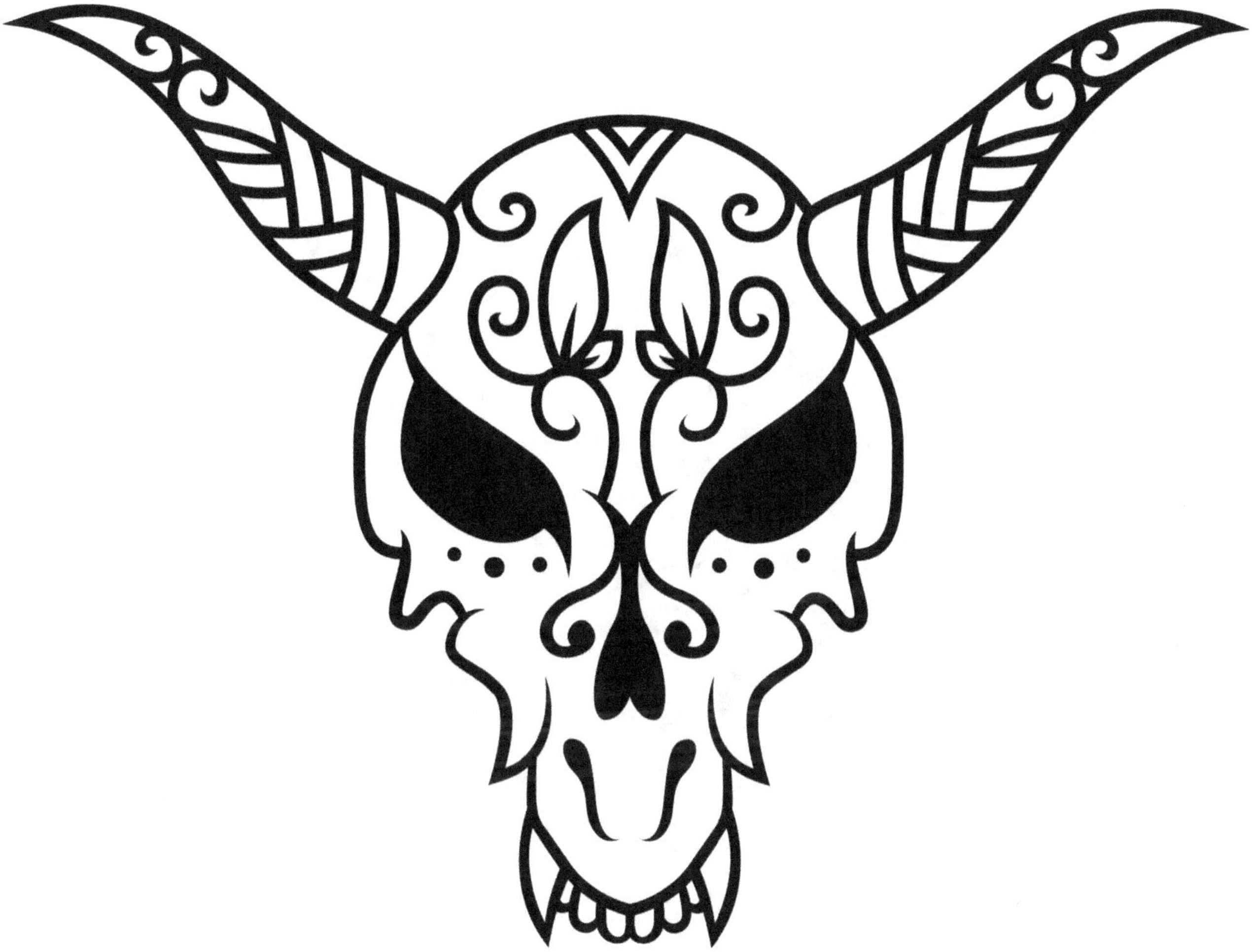

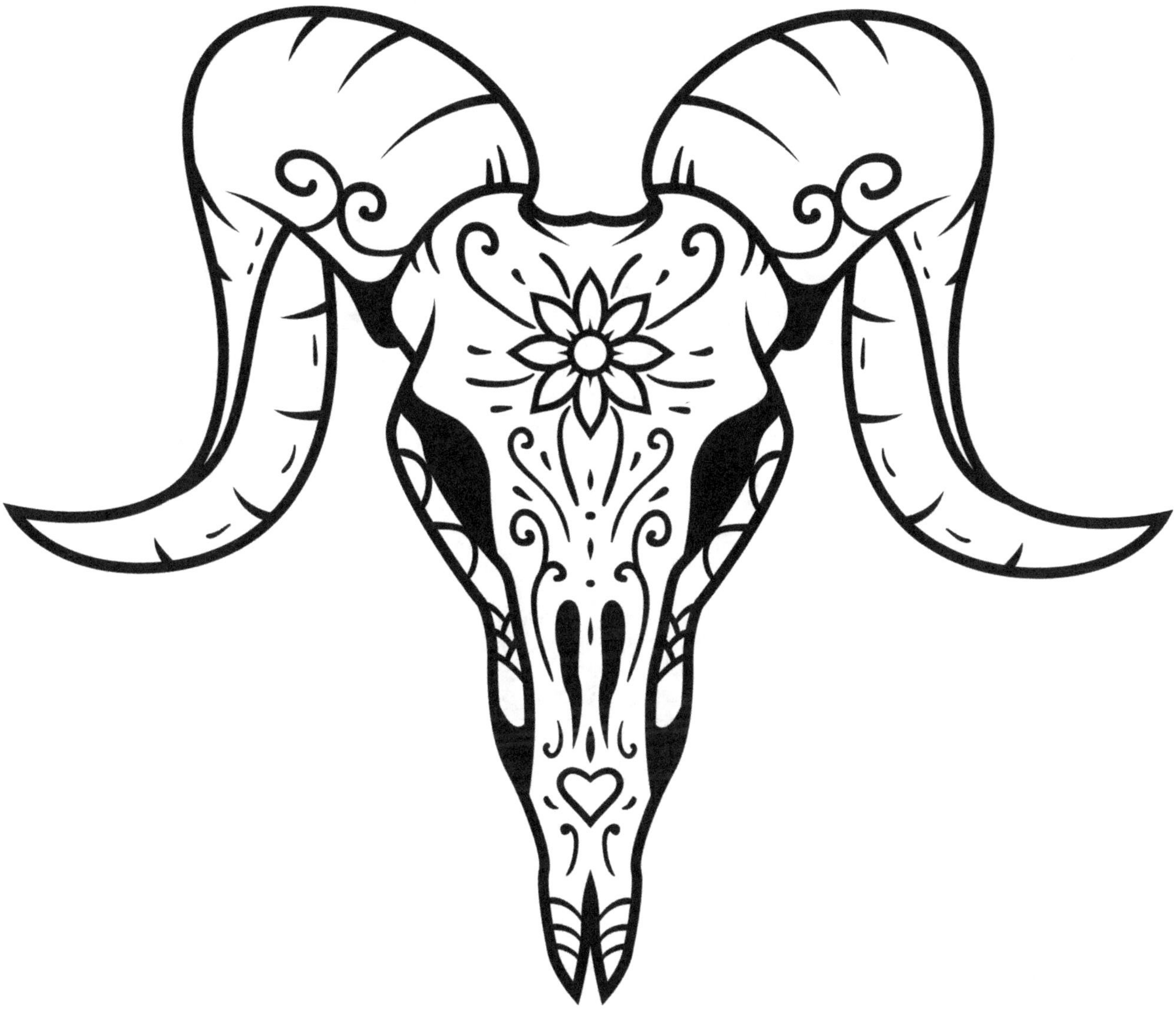

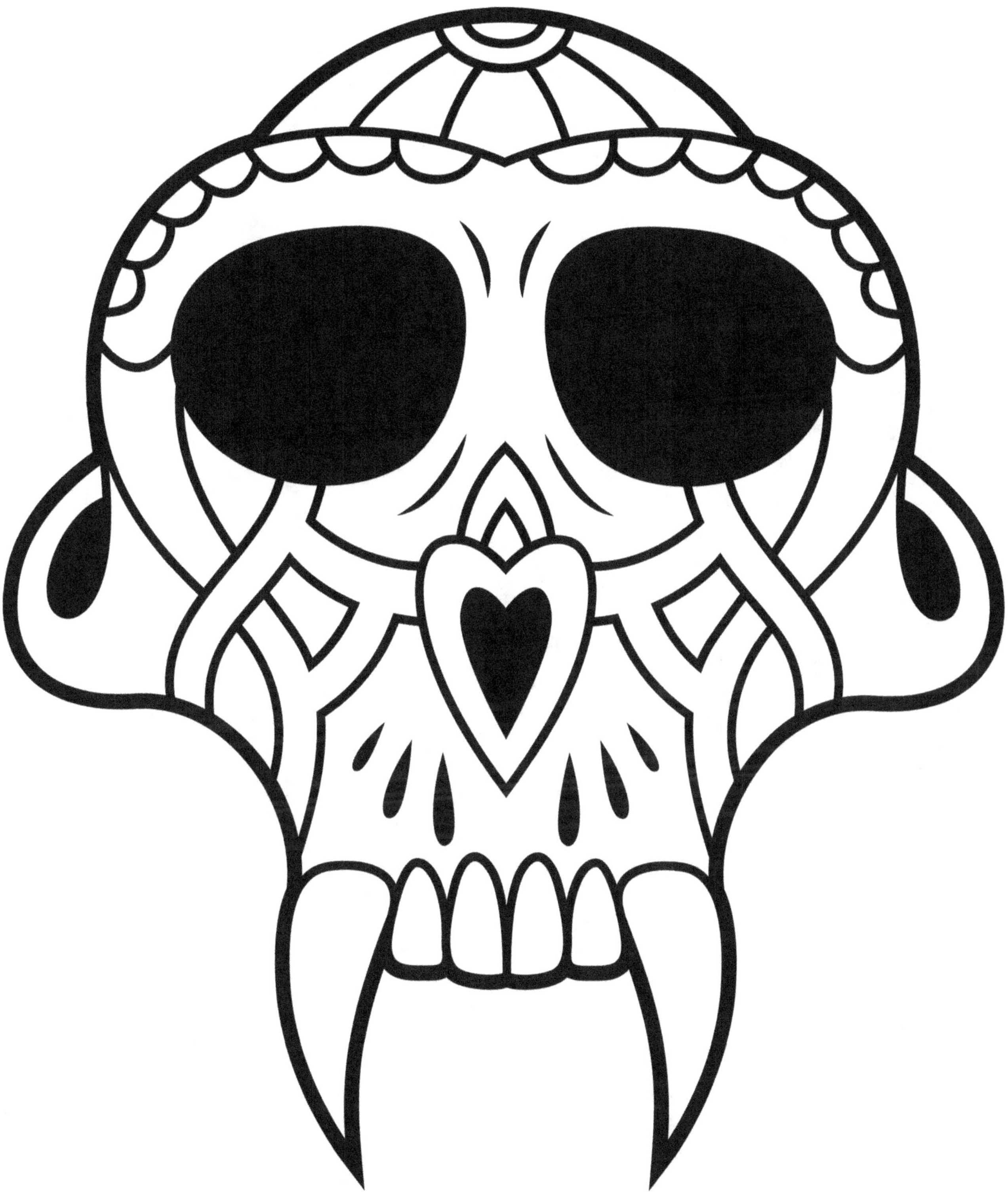

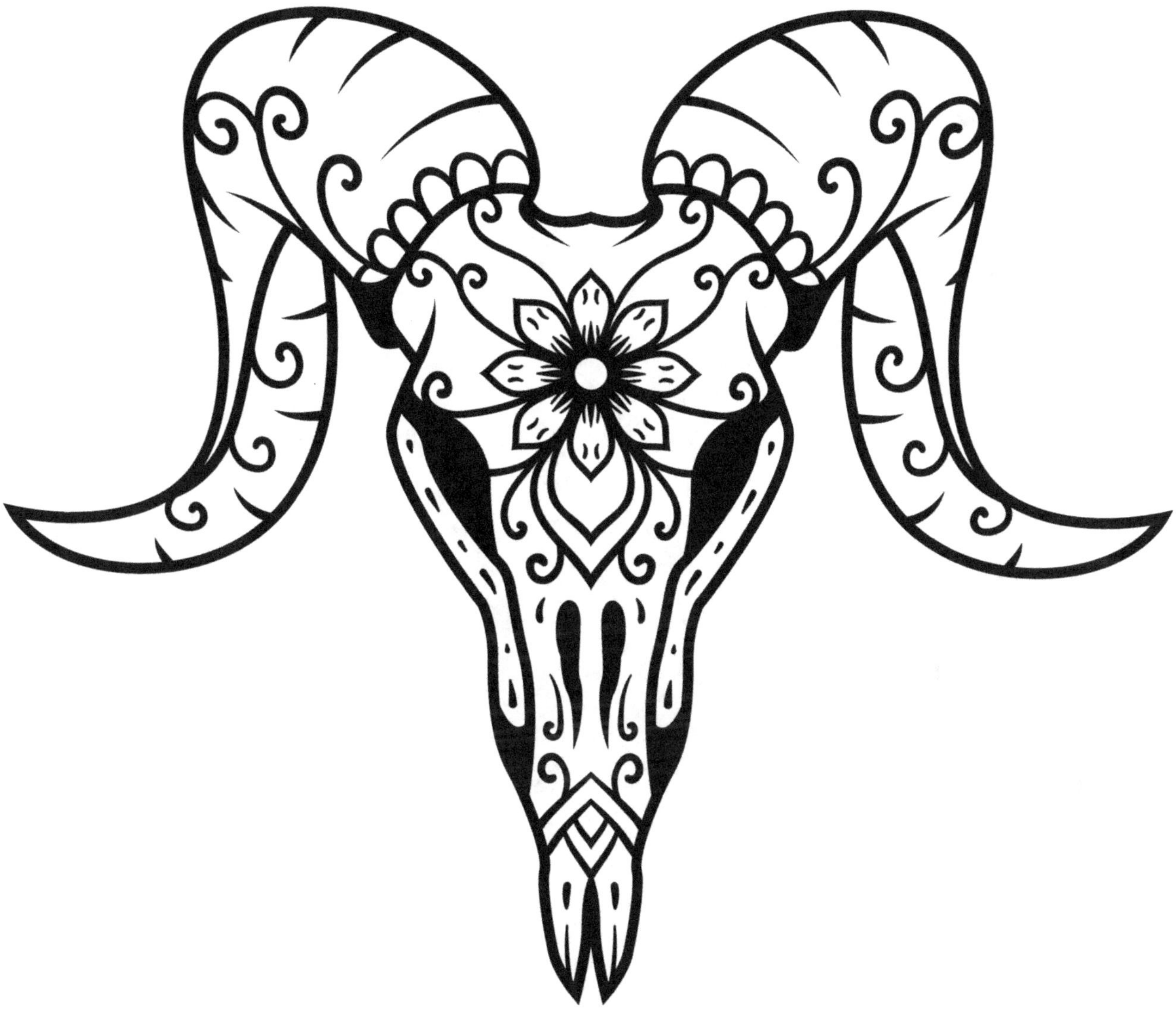

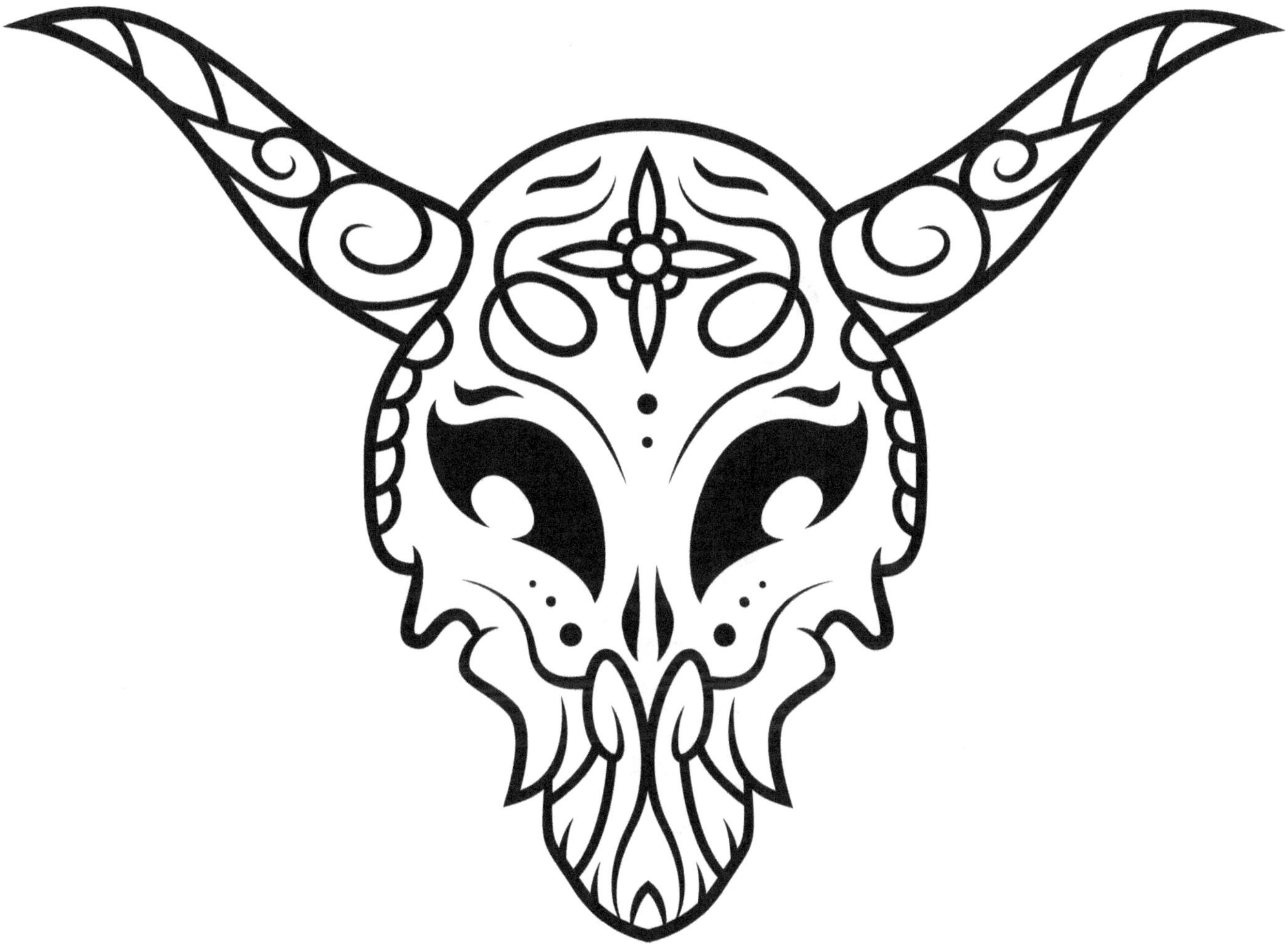

www.ingramcontent.com/pod-product-compliance
Lightning Source LLC
Chambersburg PA
CBHW081449220526
45466CB00008B/2571